PAUL ATTERBURY

AN A–Z OF RAILWAYS

A NOSTALGIC TOUR
OF BRITAIN'S RAILWAYS

D&C
David and Charles

DAY EXCURSIONS
By sea
FROM WEYMOUTH

CHANNEL ISLANDS
Guernsey and Jersey
FRANCE Cherbourg
No Passport

1962

SOUTHERN
British Railways

THE
"GOLDEN ARROW
LIMITED"

WORLD FAMOUS
DE LUXE PULLMAN
SERVICE DAILY
BETWEEN LONDON
[VICTORIA] AND
PARIS [NORD]

PARIS
6½
HOURS

Copies of the illustration
above, in colour, price 1'- and
Jig Saw puzzles 5'- each post
free from S.R.Advertising Dept.
Waterloo Station, London, S.E.1.
and through Mess's W.H.Smith's
bookstalls & shops.

SOUTHERN RAILWAY
KEY TO THE CONTINENT

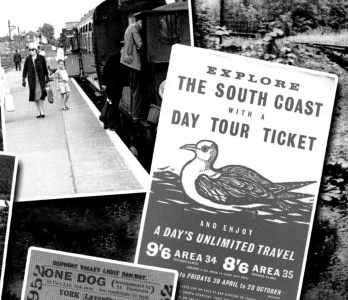

MOAT LANE JUNCTION
CHANGE FOR
LLANIDLOES RHAYADER
BUILTH WELLS BRECON
AND SOUTH WALES

DERWENT VALLEY LIGHT RAILWAY.

NONE DOG (Accompanied by)
(by Passenger)
At Co's Ltd. risk rate: see conditions on back

YORK (Layerthorpe) to

For one journey only in points. This ticket is
available for a single Journey only.
Must be given up at destination station.

FARE 6d.

952

EXPLORE
THE SOUTH COAST
WITH A
DAY TOUR TICKET

AND ENJOY
A DAY'S UNLIMITED TRAVEL

9'6 AREA 34   8'6 AREA 35
SECOND CLASS   SECOND CLASS

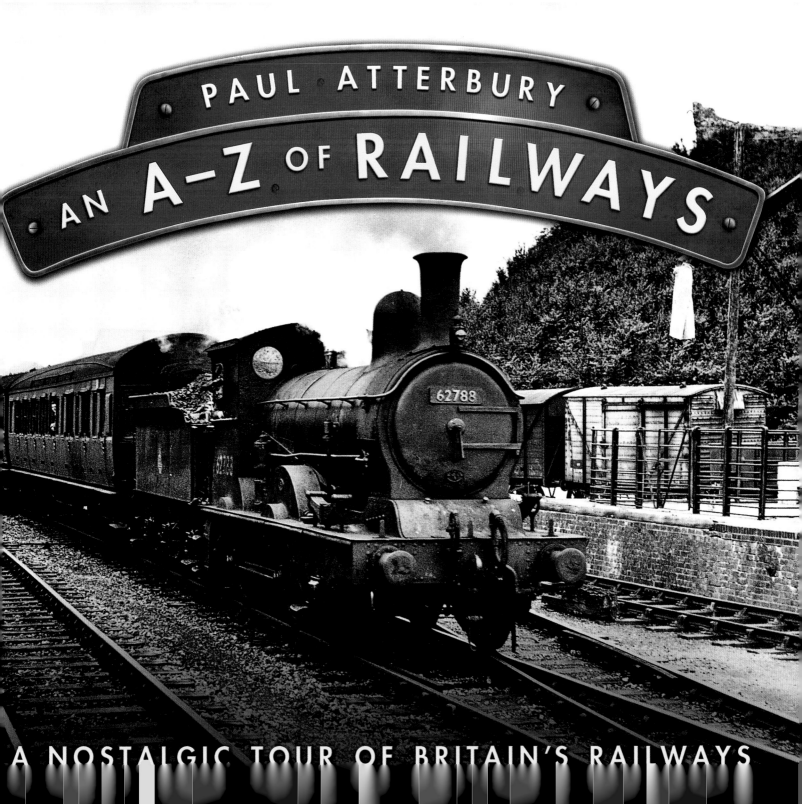

PAUL ATTERBURY

AN A-Z OF RAILWAYS

A NOSTALGIC TOUR OF BRITAIN'S RAILWAYS

CONTENTS

A DAVID & CHARLES BOOK

Copyright © David & Charles Limited 2010

David & Charles is an F+W Media, Inc. company
4700 East Galbraith Road
Cincinnati, OH 45236

First published in the UK in 2010

Copyright © Paul Atterbury 2010

Paul Atterbury has asserted his right to be identified as author of this work in accordance with the Copyright, Designs and Patents Act, 1988.

Entries in this collection were originally published in the following titles:

Tickets Please!, Branchline Britain, Along Lost Lines and *Along Country Lines*

The publisher has endeavoured to contact all contributors of pictures for permission to reproduce. If there are any errors or omissions please notify the publisher in writing.

A catalogue record for this book is available from the British Library.

ISBN-13: 978-0-7153-3814-8
ISBN-10: 0-7153-3814-5

Printed in China by RR Donnelley for
David & Charles, Brunel House,
Newton Abbot, Devon TQ12 4PU

Commissioning Editor: Neil Baber
Editor: Verity Muir and Alison Smith
Design: Sue Cleave and Kevin Mansfield
Production Controller: Kelly Smith
Pre Press: Natasha Jorden

David & Charles publish high quality books on a wide range of subjects.
For more great book ideas visit: **www.rubooks.co.uk**

INTRODUCTION

Even in their early days Britain's railways were associated, perhaps unexpectedly, with entertainment and education. Songs and poems were commonplace, and always popular were childrens' ABC, or A-Z books, based on the railway's infrastructure, buildings, vehicles, activities and personalities. The first of these date from the 1840s, and there have many later versions, including the one shown here, issued a century later. The choice of images for every letter is always interesting and sometimes eccentric or unexpected. This example ranges from A for Arrival to Z for Zero Hour. The ABC idea has also used for many other railway-linked publications, including the famous series of alphabetical timetables, made notably familiar by Agatha Christie's thriller, *The ABC Murders*. There is also the long-lived series of ABC lists of locomotives and rolling stock, published for generations of train spotters and railway enthusiasts by Ian Allan.

The A-Z principle can be applied to the railways themselves. The list of thousands of stations in Britain starts with Abbey and ends with Ystrad. Equally varied is the long list of names applied to locomotives, from the GWR's Abberley Hall of 1930 to the LNWR's Zygia, built in 1893.

This book, based on material drawn from the now well-known railway series, *Branch Line Britain, Along Country Lines, Tickets Please!* and *Along Lost Lines*, offers a new, and hopefully exciting, version of the railway A–Z.

▶ Railway ABC books for children date back to the early days of railways and often feature exciting and colourful illustrations. This is an example from the late 1940s.

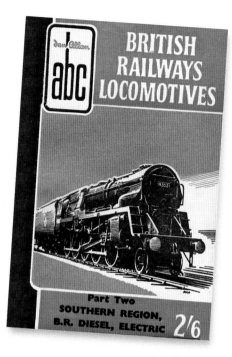

▲ British station names appeared in many shapes and styles. Particularly famous is the so-called target design issued by the Southern Railway from the 1930s. Generations of young railway enthusiasts and trainspotters grew up with the famous Ian Allan ABC series, first published in the 1940s.

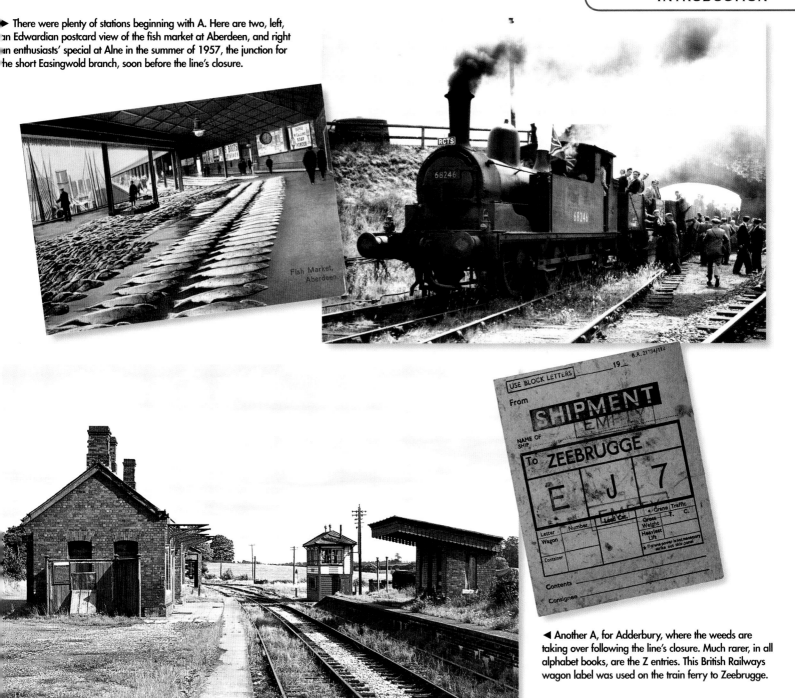

► There were plenty of stations beginning with A. Here are two, left, an Edwardian postcard view of the fish market at Aberdeen, and right an enthusiasts' special at Alne in the summer of 1957, the junction for the short Easingwold branch, soon before the line's closure.

◄ Another A, for Adderbury, where the weeds are taking over following the line's closure. Much rarer, in all alphabet books, are the Z entries. This British Railways wagon label was used on the train ferry to Zeebrugge.

AMBULANCE

In 1842 the British government decreed that the railways would be required to carry troops as needed, and through the Victorian period trains became the primary carriers of troops and equipment, usually to embarkation ports. During World War I, Southampton and other south coast ports were heavily used for shipping men and supplies to France and, for the first time, for receiving large numbers of wounded directly from battlefield dressing stations and field hospitals. There was, as a result, a huge demand for ambulance trains in both France and Britain, and many carriages were converted for this purpose. Ambulance trains ran regular services carrying the wounded directly to military and civilian hospitals, using local stations. In addition, some major hospitals, such as Netley and Lord Mayor Treloar, both in Hampshire, were served by special branch lines. In World War II, the burden on the railways was even greater, particularly after the Dunkirk evacuation and during the build-up to the D-Day invasion, and once again there was a massive requirement for ambulance trains.

► Large quantities of locomotives and rolling stock were sent from Britain to be used in France during World War I. Among these were ambulance trains built by many British railway companies to transport casualties from field hospitals to the coastal ports. This postcard shows a typical ward car, built by the Caledonian Railway.

► Many women served as nurses and medical auxiliaries during World War I, both in field hospitals near the battlefields and in the huge hospital complexes built in Britain to handle the hundreds of thousands of casualties. Popular postcard images such as this one helped to maintain the glamorous vision that these women represented in the imagination of the ordinary soldier.

▼ Ambulance trains required extensive paperwork. This World War I label from a Royal Artillery soldier's kitbag is typical of this. The soldier recovered from his wounds, and wrote on the back: 'Keep this souvenir!'

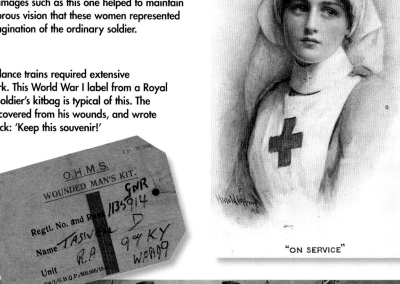

"ON SERVICE"

Interior of one of the Ward Cars of the Ambulance Train, constructed by the Caledonian Railway Company, on the order of the War Office, for conveyance of Wounded British Soldiers in France from the Front to the Sea-board.

◄ Many postcards were issued during World War I showing wounded men in their hospital wards recovering from their injuries and often, as in this case, accompanied by the nurses who looked after them. They would all have been transported by ambulance trains.

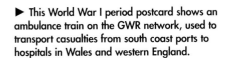

► This World War I period postcard shows an ambulance train on the GWR network, used to transport casualties from south coast ports to hospitals in Wales and western England.

◄ Lord Mayor Treloar Hospital was a large military complex near Alton, in Hampshire, with its own stop on the old Basingstoke branch. This enabled casualties to be brought to the hospital directly from the quayside in Southampton. This photograph shows the hospital's platform after the line's closure.

ARCHITECTURE

The great architectural debate of the 19th century was Gothic revival versus classical. Gothic style was successful in the first part of the 19th century because it represented a sense of history, Christianity, wealth and extravagance, industrial and imperial success, and a strong element of patriotism. Gothic was above all else perceived as a suitably British style. As a new building type, the railway station was a reflection of its age. It gloried in the stylistic confusion that Gothic and Tudor represented, but still saw it as eminently suitable for the new railway buildings of the modern age, combining history and permanence with new technology. It was also flexible; applicable alike to city termini and to country halts.

Dominant throughout the 18th century, the classical style had lost some of its appeal by the start of the railway age, partly because it was perceived by many to be pagan and thus unsuitable for a Christian country. However, its formal grandeur and elegance appealed to some early railway tycoons, mainly because it represented power, stability and permanence. For this reason, classicism was popular with

▼ This 1930s panoramic view of Gilbert Scott's majestic 1870s Midland Grand Hotel at St Pancras shows railway Gothic at its most imaginative and ambitious. With this building the Midland Railway put itself firmly on the map.

Stone

◄ The North Staffordshire Railway was adventurous in its architecture, favouring a decorative Tudor style that was the speciality of its chosen architect, Henry Hunt. Typical of this style is Stone, built in 1849, a perfect small-scale example featuring careful symmetry, contrasting brick and stone, Flemish gables and tall, decorative chimneys. Recently restored, Stone is a fine memorial to local ambition and elegance.

orthern industrialists, and therefore with some railway builders in the orth of England. Conventionally symmetrical and adhering to the rules nd orders laid down by the architecture of Greece and Rome, classicism as used in the Victorian period with considerable freedom. The building at set the standard for the pure classical style was Philip Hardwick's great ortico for Euston, wantonly destroyed in the early 1960s. This was echoed Birmingham and elsewhere but, at the same time, a more informal and laxed classicism was developed for railway stations that simply drew in a neral sense upon Italianate and Renaissance models.

▲ GT Andrews, a close associate of George Hudson, the 'railway king', designed many stations for the York & North Midland Railway and developed a characteristic domestic style of Italianate classicism for small stations. A good example is Castle Howard, built in 1845 and now a private house.

◄ With a style determined by the city it served, Bath Green Park, seen here in 1959, is a pure statement of classical symmetry. Built by the Midland Railway, completed in 1870 and closed in 1966, it was the link between the industrial north of England and the south coast.

BATH GREEN PARK

With no traditions to follow and away from the big-city style wars, the builders of rural railway stations were free to follow their own ideas. Many country stations had to combine railway functions with the domestic needs of the stationmaster or staff. Architects and builders were influenced primarily by vernacular details, materials and cost. The result is a nationwide legacy of individual and often idiosyncratic local station buildings that range from the basic to the extraordinary; a wealth of cottage-style structures that express the diversity, imagination and practicality of the railway age. Materials were often local, and decorative details could echo regional traditions. However basic, the staffed station was an outpost of the railway company it served, and its appeal to passengers was of fundamental importance. Small stations were therefore generally well maintained, with comfortable rooms, plenty of seating and fires in winter inside, while outside gardens and flowers enhanced the cottage feel.

In the early 20th century, railway companies became increasingly image conscious. This was the era of fast travel, Pullman comfort and modern marketing. Distinctive house styles and branding were part of this modernization process, all greatly accelerated by the

▲ The Darlington & Barnard Castle Railway opened in 1857, serving a remote region, with stations that looked just like cottages. This is Gainford, in stone wit barge-boarding; it has in fact been a cottage since its 1960s closure.

▼ In April 1964 tank locomotive 1445 pulls its singl carriage into Berkeley station, en route from Sharpne to Berkeley Road Junction, in Gloucestershire. A singl passenger waits, emerging from the rathe grand station, which is not unlike a lodge o a large country hous

◀ The Arts & Crafts movement of the 1900s brought vernacular details, asymmetry and domestic comfort to houses. This influential and popular style soon imposed itself on railway stations. Bexhill, built by the South Eastern & Chatham Railway at about this time, is a typical example.

▼ Rebuilt in 1961 to the designs of NG Wikeley, Chichester is a good example of postwar modernism, with plenty of details that echo the Festival of Britain. Notable are the varied use of materials, the fascia lettering and the internal light fittings.

ormation of the Big Four in 1923. Of greater mportance, however, was the major upgrading f stations and railway buildings.

In the Edwardian period, stations had egun to reflect the popularity of Arts & Crafts styles. In the 1920s, a refined and mplified classicism became fashionable, ut far more significant was the impact of odernism in the 1930s. All over the network, oncrete and geometry came together with ynamic effects as the Big Four competed their determination to present a modern

image. The GWR initiated an extensive rebuilding programme, to be seen at Cardiff, Paddington and elsewhere, but more extreme was the Southern and its architect J R Scott, who brought a distinctive Art Deco look to stations such as Bishopstone, Surbiton and those along the line to Chessington South – places that reflected the modern image of the Southern Electric network.

This was brought to an end by World War II, and by the time station rebuilding started again in the late 1950s, a new kind of modernism was emerging, with glass and metal used with brick or concrete, as seen in stations like Banbury, Harlow, Stafford, Chichester and Coventry. The 1960s were characterized by concrete brutalism, but since the post-modernist, high-tech era of the 1970s and 1980s there has been a return to more sensitive, expressive architecture.

A RT SHOW

Although stations have from the earliest days been essentially functional structures, their design and decoration often reflected the artistic ambitions of their creators. In the Victorian era decoration was mostly in stone, brick and iron, but colourful tiling and stained glass were not uncommon. Later, promotional pictures were hung in public areas such as waiting and

refreshment rooms. However, the idea of actually applying art to the walls of station buildings did not fully emerge until the late 20th century. The last years of British Rail were marked by a number of decorative painting, tiling and sculptural schemes, sometimes in conjunction with local art colleges. There have also been some endearing but largely amateur projects, usually involving supporters of a particular line or station.

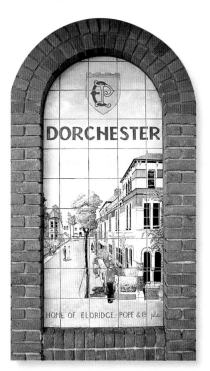

▲ Dorchester South station was rebuilt in 1986. The involvement of the local brewer, Eldridge Pope, is acknowledged in two tile panels on the new building. One shows Dorchester's High Street and the other (above) depicts part of the brewery buildings.

▶ A dull concrete wall on Wrabness station, on the Harwich branch, has been transformed by a delightful mural of waiting passengers painted in a lively, primitive manner with beautifully observed detail.

◀ The covered footbridge at Southampton Central station features a dynamic mosaic mural inspired by shipping and the port. It was designed in 1990 by Sue Ridge.

▼ In Stoke-on-Trent station, the subway is enlivened by a colourful tile mural featuring many aspects of the city's history: potteries and their ovens and products, coal mining, canals, football and the railways. Designed by local artist Liz Kayley, who worked with 200 local children, it was unveiled on 18 October 1994.

▲ In the 1980s the main staircase at Exeter St David's was decorated with a series of murals in the style of the Renaissance depicting modern railway life. Truly wonderful and eccentric, they are not now being cared for and the artist's name panel has vanished, along with its dedication: 'Thanks to Michelangelo and British Rail'.

BEECHING

The publication of the infamous report entitled *The Reshaping of British Railways* in 1963 brought the name of Dr Richard Beeching, who had become chairman of the British Transport Commission in 1961 into public prominence. Given the task of reversing the steady decline of railways in Britain, he approached the problem in a dispassionate, direct and cost-based manner. His proposal – the closure of more than 2,000 stations and thousands of miles of railway and the withdrawal of over 250 train services – caused a furore throughout the country. There were many bitter battles, but few lines scheduled for closure escaped his axe and Beeching's name became synonymous with the destruction of Britain's railways. This was in some ways unjust, for much of what Beeching recommended was inevitable. More importantly, the second part of his report, *The Development of Major Trunk Routes*, was ignored by government. Had his advice been followed, Britain could have had a modern network that the world would have envied.

► ▼ Dr Beeching's highly detailed report makes interesting reading. It addressed both freight and passenger traffic. Twelve maps supported the lists of services to be withdrawn and stations to be closed.

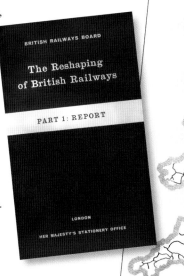

BRITISH RAILWAYS BOARD

The Reshaping of British Railways

PART 1: REPORT

LONDON

HER MAJESTY'S STATIONERY OFFICE

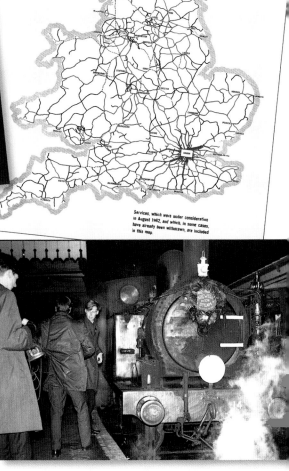

Map No.9

BRITISH RAILWAYS PROPOSED WITHDRAWAL OF PASSENGER TRAIN SERVICES

All passenger services to be withdrawn _____

All stopping passenger services to be withdrawn -------------------

Services, which were under consideration in August 1962, and which, in some cases, have already been withdrawn, are included in this map.

An objection has been received and the withdrawal of this passenger ... by the Transport Users' Consultative Committee

BRITISH RAILWAYS BOARD

PUBLIC NOTICE
TRANSPORT ACT - 1962

Withdrawal of Railway Passenger Services

The Secretary of State for the Environment has said that he is unlikely to renew the grant for the Machynlleth to Pwllheli passenger train service after the end of 1971, unless he has previously refused consent to a statutory closure proposal.

Accordingly the London Midland Region of British Railways hereby give notice in accordance with Section 56 (7) of the Transport Act 1962, that they propose to discontinue all railway passenger services between:—

MACHYNLLETH and PWLLHELI
involving the discontinuance of all passenger services from the following section of line:—

DOVEY JUNCTION — PWLLHELI

and from the following stations:—

ABERDOVEY	HARLECH	PENRHYNDEUDRAETH
ABERERCH	LLANABER	PENYCHAIN
ABERTAFOL	LLANBEDR & PENSARN	PORTMADOC
BARMOUTH	LLANDANWG	PWLLHELI
BLACK ROCK	LLANDECWYN	TALSARNAU
CRICCIETH	LLANGELYNIN	TALWRN BACH
DOVEY JUNCTION	LLWYNGWRIL	TALYBONT
DYFFRYN ARDUDWY	MINFFORDD	TONFANAU
FAIRBOURNE	MORFA MAWDDACH	TOWYN
GOGARTH	PENHELIG	TYGWYN

It appears to the Board that the following alternative services will be available:—

EXISTING SERVICES BY RAIL — NONE AVAILABLE

EXISTING SERVICES BY ROAD — Crosville Motor Services Ltd.,
Service No. 826/27 PWLLHELI & MAENTWROG
Service No. 535 MAENTWROG & BARMOUTH
Service No. 534 BARMOUTH & DOLGELLAU
Service No. 52B DOLGELLAU & TOWYN
Service No. 52A TOWYN & MACHYNLLETH

Any users of the rail service which it is proposed to discontinue and anybody representing such users may lodge an objection in writing within six weeks of 27th MARCH 1971, i.e. not later than 8th MAY 1971, addressing the objection to:—

The Secretary, Transport Users' Consultative Committee
for the Wales and Monmouthshire Area,
22 The Chambers,
40 St. Mary's Street,
Cardiff. CF1 1YD.

If any objection is lodged the service cannot be discontinued until the Transport Users' Consultative Committee has considered the objections and reported to the Secretary of State for the Environment and the Secretary has given consent to the Closure under Section 56 (8) of the Transport Act 1962

The Committee may hold a meeting to hear objections. Such a meeting will be held in public and any persons who have lodged an objection in writing may also make oral representations to the Committee.

If no objections are lodged to the proposal the service will be discontinued and the stations closed on 4th October 1971.

◄ Public Notices announcing the proposed closure of lines and stations became commonplace through the 1960s and into the 1970s. This one, dated 1971, proposed a closure that did not take place; the line is still open.

► Prior to Beeching, line closures had attracted little attention, but afterwards every one aroused great interest, and images of last trains became all too familiar. This one is at Ryde Esplanade, on the Isle of Wight, on New Year's Eve, 1966.

▼ A familiar sight all over Britain in the 1960s was the work of the demolition gangs, removing track and infrastructure following closure. This is near Notgrove, Gloucestershire, in May 1964.

◄ A curious byproduct of the Beeching era is that his name is commemorated on minor roads all over Britain, usually on housing estates built on the sites of former stations. This recent example is on the site of Wisbech St Mary station.

MERRYMAKER
Last Ride
on the
Wallingford Branch
Sunday 31 May 1981
£5·50 2nd class   £8 1st class

We are going to have a jolly 'wake' on Sunday 31 May to mark the closure of the Wallingford branch line. A special train will leave London Paddington at approx. 10 00 hours and run via Aylesbury, Claydon Jcn., Bicester, Oxford (break for refreshments) then for a final ride on the branch line, before returning through Reading to Paddington.

Accommodation limited, make sure of a place for the 'Wallingford Wake' by applying early for your tickets to:

Chief Booking Clerk
No.1 Platform,British Rail Western
Paddington,LONDON W7.

This is the age of the train ≷

▲ Most closures had happened by the early 1970s, but the Beeching legacy lingered on. One of the last, at this stage seen by British Rail as something to celebrate, was the Wallingford branch, in 1981.

BOAT TRAINS

Railway companies began to operate trains to connect with shipping services in the 1840s, initially in Scotland and for cross-Channel sailings from Dover and Folkestone. However, the vaguaries of tides made it impossible to schedule regular services, a problem not fully overcome until the 1880s, when deep-water harbours were constructed. The first dedicated boat train in Britain to operate to a fixed timetable was the Irish Mail. By the early 20th century the boat train had become quite common, and many companies ran special services to Channel, Irish and North Sea ports, to Liverpool, to Fishguard and elsewhere. Some were given suitable names, such as the Hook Continental, the American Express or the Manxman. In many cases, special carriages were used, with Pullman-style comfort and full catering facilities.

The boat train was probably at its peak in the 1920s and 1930s but some services survived until the 1980s, albeit in

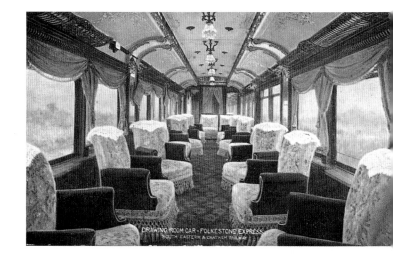

DRAWING ROOM CAR - FOLKESTONE EXPRESS
SOUTH EASTERN & CHATHAM RAILWAY

AFTERNOON TEA IN THE SALON-DE-LUXE
L. & N.W. AMERICAN SPECIAL.

◄ British Railways operated freight-only train ferries from Dover and Harwich, as this 1960s brochure indicates. Services continued until the opening of the Channel Tunnel.

a comparatively basic form. Boat trains also ran to service specific trans-Atlantic liners, such as the *Queen Mary* at Southampton. Much rarer were train ferries, transporting railway vehicles across stretches of water. First used on the Forth and the Tay, these did not become common until World War I. Freight was the prime user but from 1936 the Night Ferry carried sleeping cars between Dover and Dunkirk.

BRITISH RAILWAYS DAILY SERVICES VIA DOVER–DUNKERQUE HARWICH–ZEEBRUGGE

British Rail | Shipping Services

◀ Edwardian elegance in the drawing room car of the Folkestone Express, a regular boat train operated by the South Eastern & Chatham Railway from London Victoria.

◀ This LNWR promotional postcard of about 1910 shows ladies enjoying afternoon tea in the Salon-de-Luxe on the American Express, a scheduled boat-train service between London and Liverpool.

BOAT TRAINS

◀ In 1956 the Cunarder comes to rest at Cunard's passenger reception area in Southampton docks, having run non-stop from Waterloo. The train included Pullmans and ample baggage cars.

▼ The traditional boat train was re-introduced in 1980 by the Venice Simplon-Orient-Express. Here, in 1991, the long rake of restored Pullman cars approaches Folkestone harbour.

BOMB DAMAGE

The railway network was a natural target and German bombers did their best to bring it to a standstill. Throughout World War II there were over 10,000 attacks on the railways and between 1940 and 1942, severe damage was caused almost on a daily, or rather, nightly basis. Stations and other railway buildings were hit, bridges, viaducts, junctions and signalling were damaged or destroyed, and services were regularly interrupted. However, in most cases the damage was quickly repaired. During the famous raid on Coventry on 14 November 1940, 122 railway installations were damaged, with one three-mile section of line receiving 40 direct hits. Yet before the end of the month everything was back to normal. Near London, one two-mile stretch of line was attacked 92 times in nine months. This was the pattern throughout the country but, thanks to adequate preparation, skilled engineering, improvisation and the dedication of the staff, the trains usually kept running, despite serious manpower shortages and problems caused by the blackout.

▲ Paddington's post office and booking office were hit by a German bomb on 17 April 1941. All of London's main stations were attacked but none were permanently closed. Inevitably London and the south-east of England fared the worst: the Southern Railway experienced 170 incidents for every 100 miles of route.

▼ During World War II many stations were damaged, especially around London, and railways were regularly attacked in the hope that lines of communication would be cut. This scene of devastation greeted staff at London's St Pancras after a raid in 1942. Within days the station was back to normal.

CAMPING COACHES

Since the dawn of railways, old carriages and wagons have been used as store rooms, waiting rooms and, frequently, homes. However, the idea of using elderly or redundant carriages specifically for camping purposes did not emerge until 1933, when the London & North Eastern Railway put a batch of converted coaches on to sidings at various sites in eastern England. The LMS, the GWR and the SR rapidly followed suit, and by 1939 more than 430 carriages were scattered over England, Wales and Scotland, placed at popular seaside resorts or at remote inland or coastal spots, to be let by the week to families or groups of friends. Well converted, equipped and maintained, and offering a relatively cheap holiday, the coaches proved very popular.

During the war, camping coaches were withdrawn, but they reappeared in the 1950s, many with more modern facilities. The most luxurious were some Pullman cars converted in the 1960s. However, by then patterns of family holidays were changing, and some of the most popular sites vanished under the Beeching axe. The last camping coaches disappeared at the end of the 1971 season.

▼ The first camping coaches had no internal corridors, which made life difficult, especially in wet weather. By the late1930s, more spacious and convenient layouts had been developed. This shows the internal plan of a six-berth camping coach in use on the Eastern Region in the late 1950s. There were variations: Southern Region coaches, for example, had beds side by side rather than bunks.

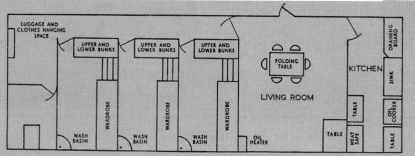

CAMPING COACHES
FULLY EQUIPPED FOR 8 PERSONS
SITUATED AT NUMEROUS ATTRACTIVE SEASIDE AND COUNTRY SITES. IDEAL FOR FAMILY HOLIDAYS
AVAILABLE 30th MARCH TO 19th OCTOBER. 1957
REDUCED CHARGES - EARLY AND LATE SEASON
ASK FOR ILLUSTRATED FOLDER AT STATIONS AND ENQUIRY OFFICES OR APPLY TO CHIEF COMMERCIAL MANAGER. WESTERN REGION. PADDINGTON STATION. LONDON. W.2

WESTERN **BRITISH RAILWAYS** REGION

▲ Camping coaches were always widely promoted by the railway companies. Posters, in characteristic colours, highlighted the levels of comfort and the splendours of the setting. This Western Region scene, somewhere in Wales, depicts a few of the qualities of a holiday in a camping coach.

► This photograph shows ⸱ living room ⸱ one of the Southern ⸱ailway's first camping ⸱oaches, taken to promote ⸱e 1936 season. ⸱e wireless, curtains, ⸱l lamp and heater all ⸱nderline the marketing ⸱epartment's claim that ⸱e coaches 'contain ⸱verything that a camper ⸱ould require'. Headed ⸱amp on Wheels', ⸱e caption goes on: 'The ⸱ilway company ⸱ave selected sites on the ⸱eauty spots of the South ⸱oast to establish these ⸱xury camps.'

▲ Through the 1950s and into the 1960s, British Railways issued brochures to promote camping coaches nationwide. The standard eight-page folder included a location map, price schedule, booking form and illustrations of scenes of camping-coach life. In 1957 weekly hire fees ranged from £5 10s to £11 10s depending on the location, the number of berths and the time of year. The leaflet stipulated that a set number of the party must travel to and from the location by train.

◄ Issued by the LNER publicity machine in 1935, this photograph illustrates the pleasures of camping-coach life 'at a secluded spot in Essex adjoining the LNER station at Southminster'. In most camping coaches, water was either pumped by hand or brought in daily in cans. Campers generally made use of the lavatories on the station platform. In many cases, daily supplies of food were delivered by train.

CAR TRAINS

On the first railways, horse-drawn carriages were transported on flat trucks, and later in covered wagons. This continued until the Edwardian era, when motor cars were first carried, notably by the Midland Railway from 1904. The Great Western also carried cars from 1909, on special services through the Severn Tunnel. However, it was not until the 1930s that the network saw regular long-distance services that carried both cars and passengers, notably between London and Scotland. Services were greatly expanded from the 1950s and by the 1960s the scheduled routes included London to several Scottish destinations, London to Cornwall, London to Fishguard, Newcastle to the West Country, the Midlands to Scotland, York to Inverness and Scotland to Newhaven. By then, 100,000 cars were being carried each year by Motorail, the name used to promote the network. Services declined rapidly from the 1980s.

▲ One of a series of promotional postcards issued by British Rail Motorail network in the 1970s, this shows a summer scene on a We Country service, with the typical flat trucks then in use

▼ The world's first all-line car train terminal was opened b Motorail at Kensington Olympia on 24 May 1966, offerin services to many parts of Britain. There were specia passenger lounges and all loading wo under cove

Motorail used a variety of vehicles for car transport, including these standard flat trucks and dedicated two-tier carriers, photographed at Carlisle Citadel station in July 1970.

▲ The Great Western began to carry cars through the Severn Tunnel in 1909, and this service remained popular with drivers wanting to avoid the long route round the Severn estuary. This 1962 leaflet offered daily services.

British Rail Car-Carrying Services 1966

Get there sooner — take your car by train

◄ A British Rail 1966 brochure includes details of all day and sleeper car-carrying services then available, most of which operated from May to September. Among the unusual routes were Sutton Coldfield to Stirling, Newton-le-Willows to Newton Abbot, Stirling or Leeds to Newhaven and York to Inverness. There were also connections with ferries to France and Ireland.

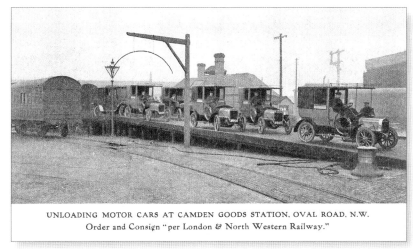

UNLOADING MOTOR CARS AT CAMDEN GOODS STATION, OVAL ROAD, N.W.
Order and Consign "per London & North Western Railway."

▲ This promotional card issued by the London & North Western Railway in the Edwardian era shows the early days of car carrying.

CLOSURES

It has always been for economic reasons that railway lines and stations have been closed. The first recorded withdrawal of passenger services took place in 1833; by 1920, by which time parliamentary assent was required before lines could be closed, some 400 miles had gone. As the network had been built up piecemeal by rival private companies, many routes were duplicated. After the formation of the Big Four in 1923, with increased competition from buses and the loss of freight traffic to road haulage, the closure process accelerated, and a further 1,650 miles had gone by 1947, a fifth of these being in Scotland. In some cases lines closed to passengers were kept open for freight. Closures mostly affected branch lines but some through routes were also axed, the longest being the 36-mile line from Alnwick to Coldstream, which went in 1930.

Dr Richard Beeching became Chairman of British Railways in 1962 and his famous 1963 report addressed, for the first time from a national point of view, the problems faced by the network. The report's recommended closure of 280 routes and 1,850 stations was carried out throughout the 1960s and early 1970s. What is forgotten today is that the report also planned a future for the network based on integration and public funding.

▶ A familiar sight in the 1960s were notices at stations announcing line closures, a necessary part of the legal process. This example, complete with black mourning bows, announces the end of the Somerset & Dorset in 1966.

▼ Probably the last significant line closure in Britain was the Haltwhistle to Alston branch, in March 1976. This view shows Featherstone Park station, a minor halt on the route north of Lambley. The last train has passed, the crowds have dispersed and soon the demolition men will arrive to remove all those things that made it a working railway.

◢ Closure is followed by the busy process of demolition. In 1964 this was under way at Andoversford Junction, where the Banbury to Cheltenham line met the Midland & South Western Junction's route to Cheltenham via Swindon, a typical Beeching casualty.

► Some regions were particularly hard hit by the 1960s closures, for example East Anglia. At Melton Constable, once the heart of the extensive Midland & Great Northern network, lines have gone and buildings are derelict. Today only the water tower on the right remains.

◄ Some closed lines do re-open. Here, crowds have gathered on 3 November 1956 to see the last train on the Welshpool & Llanfair Railway, little dreaming that it would later be revived as a tourist line, preserved by volunteers.

CRASHES

Railway accidents are as old as railways, and people have been killed by trains since the 18th century. The three main causes of accidents have been: technical failure of equipment, inadequate operational control, and human error. The first of these, with results ranging from exploding boilers to collapsing bridges, became steadily rarer as technology improved. The second, at its most common during the rapid growth of the network before the 1870s, was brought under better control by constant improvements in communications, signalling technology and vehicle braking. Human error, unfortunately, remains unpredictable and ever present, although modern technology, such as Automatic Train Protection, increasingly takes the decision-making and control out of human hands. In the early 1840s the government, mindful of public concern about the frequency of accidents and the lack of response from

▲ One of Britain's most mysterious accidents took place at Grantham, Lincolnshire, late on 19 September 1906. A train bound for Edinburgh, due to stop at Grantham, swept through the station at speed and was derailed. The dead included the train crew, so the cause was never established.

◀ Every accident, however minor, has to be fully investigated. This is the report into a minor collision at Portsmouth on 15 December 1971, caused by a driver passing a red signal at slow speed.

▼ On 10 November 1946 a permanent-way failure derailed the 4.45pm Newcastle to Kings Cross express at Marshmoor, in Hertfordshire.

DEPARTMENT OF THE ENVIRONMENT

RAILWAY ACCIDENT

Report on the Collision
that occurred on 15th December 1971
at Portsmouth & Southsea Station

IN THE
SOUTHERN REGION
BRITISH RAILWAYS

LONDON, HER MAJESTY'S STATIONERY OFFICE
1972
51p net

railway companies, introduced the first of a series of Parliamentary Acts that established an independent inspectorate to investigate all railway accidents and make recommendations in their reports. The worst accident in British railway history took place in Quintinshill, near Gretna Green, in 1915, involving five trains and 227 deaths. Human error was the cause but fires in the gaslit wooden carriages exacerbated the result.

Postcard publishers were fascinated by train crashes. This one shows the wreck of the Plymouth to Waterloo boat train at Salisbury, following the crash late on 30 June 1906, which killed 28 people. It was caused by the driver ignoring the 30mph speed limit through Salisbury station and going through at at least 60mph. The train derailed east of the station and crashed into a milk train. Amazingly the locomotive, shown here, was later driven away.

◄ Many accidents are minor and do not involve any loss of life or injuries. This Edwardian photograph shows some derailed wagons at Dawlish, in Devon.

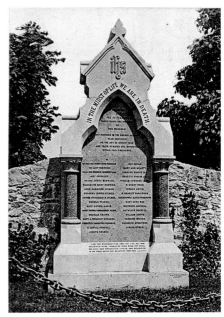

On 1 September 1905 the 9.27am Liverpool Street to Cromer express was derailed at high speed at Witham, Essex, by a loose rail, the result of careless track maintenance. Parts of the station were demolished. This postcard, sent from Norwich just over two weeks later, makes no mention of the accident. However, it shows how quickly the cards could be issued.

▲ One of the worst crashes in the Victorian era took place at Abergele, in north Wales, on 20 August 1868, when the Irish Mail collided at speed with some runaway goods wagons that included paraffin tankers. The public horror at the disaster inspired this memorial to the victims of the accident.

DAY TRIPS

Railway companies began running special trains from the 1830s. These were most notably for those attending race meetings but other, earlier users of these services were temperance and religious societies and mechanics' institutes. By the 1840s these specials had become both widespread and regular, and so the excursion train was born. In 1844, for example, the London & Brighton Railway began to operate regular excursions along its route, seeing this as a profitable way to increase business. Other companies followed, and the traffic increased steadily, particularly at Easter and in the summer. Excursions could be day trips over short distances or longer journeys taking many hours, with participants sleeping on the train. The emergence of

► By the 1970s excursions were sometimes just a means of encouraging weekend travel, in this case from Oxenholme in May 1974.

▲ This 1950s BR leaflet offers excursions from Paddington to Oxford and Blenheim Palace, including the 'road conveyance'. Tea was available at Blenheim for an extra cost.

the travel agent greatly expanded excursion traffic, despite the fact that the carriages used were often primitive, uncomfortable and overcrowded.

Excursions were run for all sorts of reasons. In 1849 an excursion train from London carried its passengers to Norwich to watch a public execution. The Bank Holiday Act of 1871 brought a further increase in excursion traffic, by which time standards of safety and comfort had been greatly improved.

▲ Edwardian holidaymakers, using a scheduled service for a seaside excursion, descend from a GWR railcar for a day at Dawlish Warren, in Devon. Typically well dressed, they probably used the special day-outing excursion fares that were offered by many railway companies.

◄ Happy children and ladies in flowery frocks seem to be enjoying their outing to the biscuit factory, as they pose by no. 4937 'Lanelay Hall', the GWR locomotive that has brought them to Reading on a sunny day in the 1930s.

► Excursions to railway workshops have long been popular. Southampton docks and Swindon works on the same trip must have seemed good value to the trainspotters on this 1962 outing.

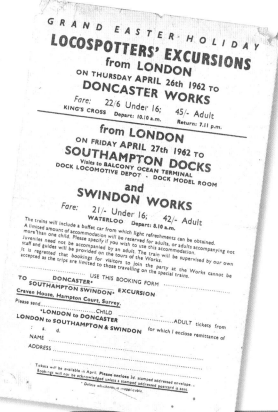

GRAND EASTER HOLIDAY
LOCOSPOTTERS' EXCURSIONS
from LONDON
ON THURSDAY APRIL 26th 1962 TO
DONCASTER WORKS

Fare: 22/6 Under 16; 45/- Adult
KING'S CROSS Depart: 10.10 a.m. Return: 7.11 p.m.

from LONDON
ON FRIDAY APRIL 27th 1962 TO
SOUTHAMPTON DOCKS
Visits to BALCONY OCEAN TERMINAL
DOCK LOCOMOTIVE DEPOT · DOCK MODEL ROOM
and
SWINDON WORKS

Fare: 21/- Under 16; 42/- Adult
WATERLOO Depart: 8.10 a.m.

The trains will include a buffet car from which light refreshments can be obtained. A limited amount of accommodation will be reserved for adults, or adults accompanying not more than one child. Please specify if you wish to use this accommodation. Juveniles need not be accompanied by an adult. The train will be supervised by our own staff and guides will be provided on the tours of the Works. It is regretted that bookings for visitors to join the party at the Works cannot be accepted as the trips are limited to those travelling on the special trains.

USE THIS BOOKING FORM
TO DONCASTER*
SOUTHAMPTON SWINDON* EXCURSION
Craven House, Hampton Court, Surrey.

Please send ....
*LONDON to DONCASTER ....CHILD
LONDON to SOUTHAMPTON & SWINDON ....ADULT tickets from
for which I enclose remittance of
£ s. d.
NAME ....
ADDRESS ....

Tickets will be available in April. Please enclose 3d. stamped addressed envelope. Bookings will not be acknowledged unless a stamped addressed postcard is sent.
* Delete whichever is inapplicable.

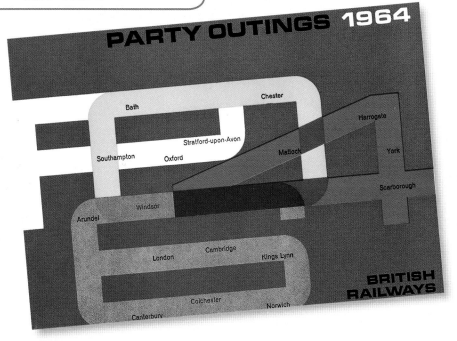

◀ Dynamic design underlines British Railways' promotion of party outings in this 1964 brochure. Inside are many suggestions for an organized party using scheduled services – a Thames cruise, Constable country, Coventry Cathedral, Lorna Doone country, the Wye Valley, Blackpool's seaside, Scottish islands, even no-passport trips to the Continent. The party organize travels free, provided there are 25 taking part, and party catering offers packed meals in carrier bags or a small meal tray.

▲ Many railway companies encouraged people to use their excursion trains by publishing postcards of scenic destinations on their routes, in this case Wastwater, accessible from the Furness Railway's Seascale station.

At the same time, companies began to take their employees on outings to the seaside. A famous example was the Great Western Railway's annual Swindon Trip; in July 1914, 26,000 people left the town for the day. Excursions and outings remained a major railway business throughout the 1920s and 1930s, with sporting events and seaside trips heading the popularity table. After nationalization, excursions began to diminish, although they retained their popularity on a more local level and continued to be promoted through the 1970s and early 1980s, many combining rail travel with road or sea outings, or with entrance to exhibitions, museums or country houses. At the same time, party travel was increasingly promoted to encourage small groups to use regular services instead of special or excursion trains. Today, dedicated excursion trains

◀ The train has pulled into the platform at Blackpool Central and a crowd of day trippers amble towards the exit. In late Victorian and Edwardian England, Blackpool was an immensely popular resort, catering for holidaymakers from the industrial towns of Lancashire. In the season, long holiday excursion trains awaited their turn at the crowded platforms, each one pouring its hundreds of remarkably well-dressed visitors into the town and its pubs and on to its beaches and amusements. Each night the whole process was reversed.

◀ Excursions were often organized and promoted by magazines and newspapers. Here, those taking part in an excursion organized by the *Stroud News* in about 1910 assemble at Stroud station, in Gloucestershire.

Outings organized by companies for their employees in all areas of business were common from the 1860s. Railway employees also made the most of outings and excursions. Here, a group of LNER commercial managers enjoy a day at sea in the summer of 1929.

C.M. OUTING 15.6.29.

DINING ON BOARD

Until the 1870s, refreshments were only available from stations, and stops on the journey were often chaotic as passengers struggled to eat or buy supplies for the journey. The development of corridor-connected carriages made restaurant cars possible. The first example was a modified American-style Pullman introduced by the Great Northern Railway in 1879. Other companies quickly followed and soon specially built restaurant and kitchen cars were in widespread use. Many restaurant cars had a bar area, but more informal buffet cars appeared from 1899.

The heyday of the restaurant car was probably from the 1920s to the 1960s, when they were attached as a matter of course to many services, and were available to different classes of ticket holders. It was at this point that the railway breakfast became a famous part of the British train experience. Today, few railway companies operate a full restaurant car

service with on-board cooking and most passengers have to put up with bar service or the ubiquitous trolley. The self-contained sleeping car, with individual berths, proper bedding and lavatory facilities, first appeared in 1873, and then became universal on longer routes.

◄ Luncheon is being served in the third-class restaurant and bar car on a GWR train out of London in 1946.

◄ In 1946, as train travel returned to normal after World War II, British Railways began to promote its sleeper and restaurant services. Many operated together, to enable sleeping car passengers to enjoy a nightcap or a full breakfast. Here, a remarkably fresh-looking sleeping car passenger receives her early morning tea tray.

► The Hungry Traveller, issued by British Railways in the late 1950s, promoted all rail catering facilities, including station refreshment rooms and bars, restaurant cars, and pre-packed meal and picnic boxes.

The Hungry Traveller

715

L. N. E. R.
SLEEPING CAR TICKET
NEWCASTLE (E.O.) to
KING'S CROSS LONDON
FIRST CLASS   Charge 12s.6d.
The holder of this Ticket must also have a First Class Railway Ticket. This Ticket must be shewn and given up when required.
NOT TRANSFERABLE
2790

◄ At the time this card was issued by the LNWR in about 1910, to promote boat-train service to Liverpool for travellers to America, kitchen cars were equipped with coal-fired stoves. The risk of fire encouraged a general move to kitchens using bottled gas and electricity from the 1920s onwards.

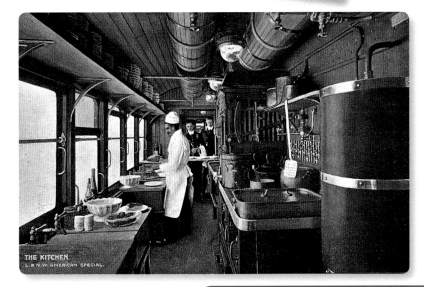

THE KITCHEN
L. & N.W. AMERICAN SPECIAL.

DOCKS AND HARBOURS

The great expansion of docks and harbours in Victorian Britain was driven directly by the spreading railway network, and from the 1840s, railway companies were actively involved in dock development. New docks were planned from the start to be served by the railway, with notable examples in Hull and London in the 1850s. At about the same time, railway companies began to appreciate the advantages of owning the docks they served, thereby having control over development, management and pricing. As a result, railways were the driving force behind the creation of many new dock complexes, with famous examples being Barrow, built from nothing by the Furness Railway, the Great Western's new docks at Millbay in Plymouth and Fishguard, and Goole, a development by the Lancashire & Yorkshire company. This pattern continued through the latter part of the Victorian era and into the 20th century. The greatest railway port was Southampton, bought by th LSWR in 1892 and massively developed by that company and its successor, the Southern Railway, to the point where it overtook Liverpool in both passenger and freight business. After the Grouping of 1923 the GWR found itself the largest dock-owning company in the world.

▲ The Falmouth branch is one of few in Cornwall to survive, kept open during the closures of the 1960s by the then still busy Falmouth harbour. Since then things have changed and Falmouth Docks station is little more than a name, a single track and its distinctive building, seen here in 1990.

◄ Glasson dock was created by the Lancaster Canal and contributed hugely to that company's success. In 1883 a branch line was built from Lancaster to serve the dock, adding to its success. This 1890s photograph shows Glasson Dock station still looking spic and span. The line closed in 1964.

▼ Kyle of Lochalsh, formerly the ferry point for the Isle of Skye, owed its development to the Highland Railway, whose long branch from Inverness finally arrived in 1897. For years it was busy with Skye traffic, and here, in 1965, there is still plenty of freight, but today the road bridge takes it all.

DOCKS AND HARBOURS

Most railway docks were for general traffic, but some handled specific products, such as coal or fish. Other harbours were linked to passenger-carrying services, notably across the Irish Sea, the English Channel and the North Sea. Alongside major dock developments, such as Grangemouth in Scotland and Grimsby and Immingham around the Humber, there were also hundreds of small ports and harbours scattered along the coastline. Many had existed for centuries but were given a new lease of life by railway connections. Wherever possible, lines were laid along ancient quays – typical examples include Pembroke, Kyle of Lochalsh, Falmouth, Rye, Brightlingsea, Looe and Whitby. In other places entirely new harbours were created by railways.

▲ This delightfully posed postcard view shows Heysham station in the Edwardian era. One of the many harbour stations built for the Irish trade and reached via Lancaster, it was never as busy as some of its rivals. At the platform is a motor train, an early example of a push-pull multiple unit.

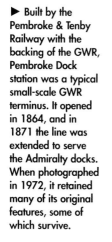

▶ Built by the Pembroke & Tenby Railway with the backing of the GWR, Pembroke Dock station was a typical small-scale GWR terminus. It opened in 1864, and in 1871 the line was extended to serve the Admiralty docks. When photographed in 1972, it retained many of its original features, some of which survive.

Modern docks with rail access were capable of handling every type of cargo, at a time when Britain was still a major exporter of manufactured goods. A typical cargo in 1924 was railway locomotives, built at the Vulcan Foundry for the Indian railways and here being loaded at Birkenhead docks.

In 1963 a diesel shunter moves a group of wagons along the quayside at Dover Eastern Docks, overlooked by Dover Castle on the horizon. At this point many docks in Britain were still primarily rail-operated. Today few quays ever see a train, though the tracks often remain, a derelict reminder of past glories.

ENGINE SHEDS

For any railway enthusiast in the steam age, Mecca was represented by the engine shed, a magic and mysterious place devoted to the servicing and maintenance of steam locomotives. All trainspotters visited sheds, usually unofficially but sometimes armed with that ever-so-desirable piece of paper, the Shed Pass. Apart from the excitement of the experience, a shed visit usually offered the chance to record a large number of locomotive sightings, including some unexpected rarities, and to underline their numbers in the *ABC* guides. There were hundreds of sheds spread over the railway network,

BRITISH RAILWAYS—OPERATIONS DEPARTMENT

RIDING OF BICYCLES ON THE BOARD'S PREMISES

Attention has been called to the practice that has arisen of Employees riding bicycles along the railway, also in and around Engine Sheds.

All members of the staff are hereby notified that this practice is forbidden.

CHIEF OPERATIONS MANAGER

BH 32109/24

◄ Worcester had a linear shed with three running tracks. In the summer of 1958 the shed was still busy. WR 6950 'Kingsthorpe Hall' stands on shed, over the ash pit. To the left is a row of stored locomotives and to the right the ubiquitous line of coal wagons. A man with the look of an enthusiast is striding out of the shed.

making them accessible to enthusiasts even in remote corners of the country.

Steam locomotives are complicated machines demanding regular servicing and constant maintenance. The shed, or motive power depot in modern parlance, enabled much of this to be carried out under cover, while at the same time offering storage for

▲ Middlesbrough shed, seen here towards the end of its life, was an example of the semi-circular type of shed, with tracks radiating from a central turntable. Iron columns support the roof.

locomotives not in use. As a result, sheds emerged in the very early days of the railways. The earliest, and the most common, was the straight type, with parallel tracks, inspection pits and access from both ends. Their advantage was that they were relatively easy to construct and extend, and could house a large number of locomotives. The GWR's Swindon shed of the 1840s could hold 48.

Linear sheds could be of any size, right down to the little ones at the ends of branch lines, designed for a single engine. The other main type was circular or semi-circular, with tracks radiating from a central turntable. These were used where space was restricted and many, such as the Roundhouse at Camden Town, in north London, were architecturally very striking. Their disadvantage was that only one

◄ A busy mainline shed was a constant turmoil of activity. This is Cardiff's exotically named Canton shed photographed in the early 1960s, with a variety of locomotives being prepared for duty. By now the shed was firmly in British Railway's Western Region, yet it still bore the clear stamp of the old GWR.

◄ Steam haulage finished on the Southern Region in July 1967. On the last day two classic Bulleid locomotives, 34060 '25 Squadron' and 34098 'Templecombe', stand silent inside Salisbury shed, their active lives over. The scrapyard beckons.

▼ By 1967 steam was clearly on the way out, yet in March that year Crewe South shed was still full of activity as the Black Fives and a Britannia were prepared for duty. This yard also boasted a mechanical coaling tower, which dominated the skyline.

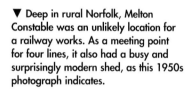

▼ Deep in rural Norfolk, Melton Constable was an unlikely location for a railway works. As a meeting point for four lines, it also had a busy and surprisingly modern shed, as this 1950s photograph indicates.

Photographs showing GWR sheds during the Victorian era are unusual. This shed's location is unknown but the identities of two locomotives can be established: 338 and 1227.

locomotive at a time could use the turntable. As a result, larger sheds often had several turntables. Early sheds were built of wood, but this soon gave way to brick and stone, and later to steel and concrete. The roofs were often partially glazed, with plenty of smoke vents.

The shed itself was used mainly for storage and servicing but also associated with the shed, and its yards, were facilities for coaling, watering, ash removal and turning. A locomotive that had been through the service procedure was said to be 'on shed' and ready for use. For decades, servicing was done largely by hand but from the 1930s mechanization brought coaling towers and ash disposal systems. Large central water tanks fed the many water columns around the shed and the yard. In some cases water and coaling towers were combined. Many sheds were equipped with workshops to enable basic maintenance to be carried out, while larger ones often had full facilities for major repairs and overhauls, along with offices and accommodation.

This is Swindon motive power depot in the 1960s, as steam was giving way to diesel. Two old Halls lurk in the shadows, while a Western and a Type 3 Hymek take the limelight.

ENGINE SHEDS

As diesel and electric locomotives began to replace steam, some sheds were adapted. However, as most were related directly to the needs of steam engines, the vast majority were closed, abandoned and often demolished. New uses were found for a few but in principle the old shed, and everything it represented, was faced with extinction. Some early or unusual roundhouses have been listed and preserved but they are no longer in use as sheds. Today the only complete large-scale steam era depot that survives in Britain, and probably in Western Europe, is Steamtown, at Carnforth, in Lancashire.

Trains still need servicing and maintaining, so a new generation of modern maintenance depots has been built by the various operating companies. Often impressive in both scale and equipment, these represent the new world of the railways in Britain, but they will never match the allure and magic of the old shed.

▲ Many sheds had occasional open days but were rarely seen as spic and span as Willesden, London, looks here, during a British Railways exhibition in June 1954.

◄ Larger sheds were equipped with full repair facilities. Here, in Perth shed in September 1961, 45483 has a major overhaul, its weight supported by the heavy lift crane.

▲ On 10 July 1967, the day after steam haulage ended on the Southern Region, the engine shed at Weymouth became a graveyard and dumping ground for many classes of once-proud, now redundant locomotives.

◄ By 1972 old steam sheds were disappearing rapidly. However, some had been taken over by the diesels. This is Gateshead, with its turntable still in place but disused. At least four classes of diesel are present, including a Deltic, D9011 'The Royal Northumberland Fusiliers'.

BR. 32709/4.

BRITISH RAILWAYS BOARD.

NOTICE.

JUMPING OVER INSPECTION PITS IS PROHIBITED.

E VACUEES

The plans to evacuate families, and particularly children, from London and other 'front line' towns and cities in the event of war had been drawn up well before the start of World War II and indeed the evacuation actually started on 1 September 1939. Many families and children, and hospital patients, were moved during the next few weeks, but this was merely a rehearsal for the main event, which happened during the summer of 1940, as the Blitz was raging. During that year 805 special trains carried nearly half a million people away from the danger areas, and thousands of city children had to come to terms with separation from their parents in an unfamiliar rural world.

Evacuations continued through 1941 but by that time many of the children had returned to their families and the whole experience had become a distant memory. In the summer of 1944, with the arrival of the V1 flying bombs and the V2 rockets, it all started again, and children were once more separated from their families and sent away from London and the Kent coast on special trains. This second evacuation was shortlived and by August it was all over, the V-weapon launch sites having been overrun by the Allied armies. The railways were the key to the success of the evacuation plans, and they handled this extra traffic successfully. However, the sight of small children standing on platforms clutching their suitcases and gas masks is one that will never be forgotten.

◀ Children were evacuated through the autumn of 1939, although the expected aerial bombardment of London and other cities had not happened. This early evacuation, in the event unnecessary, proved to be a vital rehearsal for the real thing in the summer of 1940. Here, typically well dressed children are guided on to their train by a policeman on 14 December 1939. For most of them, their stay in the country was to be brief.

◄ By the autumn of 1940 the worst of the Blitz was over but evacuations continued. By now the government had learned that the sight of small children being sent off alone could have a negative effect in propaganda terms, so the mother-and-child scheme was launched. In late September 1940, 3,500 mothers and children left London together. Some of that group are gathered here on the platform, awaiting their train under the watchful eye of the law.

▲ The bulk of the evacuation traffic was carried by the Southern Railway but all companies played their part. In 1940 the GWR carried 70,000 children in special trains from Paddington, including this group arriving at Maidenhead station. Transport to the London termini and from the destination station to distribution centres in local towns and villages was in fleets of motor buses and coaches. Thanks to careful pre-planning, the whole operation went smoothly, even if many of those taking part did not enjoy it.

FILMS

Some of the earliest films made in the 1890s feature trains, often seen from the lineside. Even more popular were sequences shot from the locomotive footplate. One of the first adventure films was about a train robbery. Since then there have been many films in which trains and railway settings play major roles. Famous 1930s examples include *Oh! Mr Porter* and *The Lady Vanishes*, while the classic of the 1940s is *Brief Encounter*. There are countless films with important railway sequences, from *Murder on the Orient Express* to James Bond. In Britain, the railway preservation movement has given film makers and television directors ample opportunities for filming railway scenes in period dramas.

► The only significant branch line film is *The Titfield Thunderbolt*, whose poster, designed by Edward Bawden, is shown here. Made in the 1950s, just as British Railways was about to devastate its local network, it tells the story of the struggle to save a branch line. A splendid social comedy, the film had many memorable performances, but the real hero was the old Liverpool & Manchester Railway locomotive, 'Lion', seen above during filming at Combe Hay, near Bath, in June 1952.

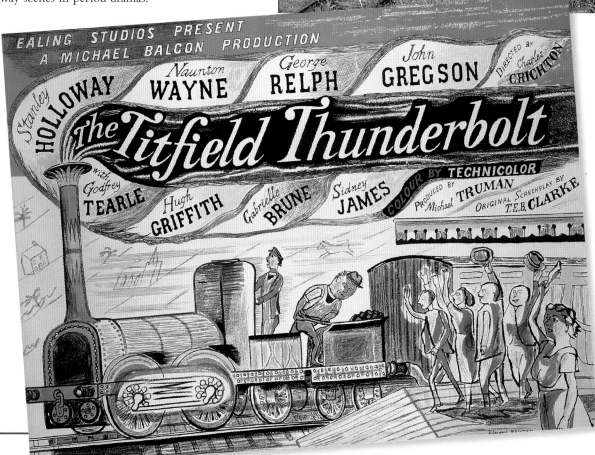

EALING STUDIOS PRESENT A MICHAEL BALCON PRODUCTION

Stanley HOLLOWAY · Naunton WAYNE · George RELPH · John GREGSON · DIRECTED BY Charles CRICHTON

The Titfield Thunderbolt

with Godfrey TEARLE · Hugh GRIFFITH · Gabrielle BRUNE · Sidney JAMES · COLOUR BY TECHNICOLOR · PRODUCED BY Michael TRUMAN · ORIGINAL SCREENPLAY BY T.E.B. CLARKE

FRANK LAUNDER and SIDNEY GILLIAT present

FRANKIE HOWERD & DORA BRYAN in

THE GREAT St. Trinian's TRAIN ROBBERY

Co-starring
George Cole
Reg Varney
Raymond Huntley
Richard Wattis

Terry Scott
Eric Barker
Godfrey Winn

EASTMAN COLOUR

◀ Loosely inspired by the real great train robbery, which took place in 1963 on the Glasgow to London Royal Mail train, this light-hearted film was filmed on the Longmoor Military Railway in Hampshire.

▼ *The Railway Children* is probably everyone's favourite railway film, judging by the number of times it appears on television. Beautifully adapted from E E Nesbit's book and filmed on the Keighley & Worth Valley Railway, the film is a railway classic. However, one has to ask what a 1930s GWR tank engine is doing in an Edwardian melodrama set in Yorkshire!

◀ Feature films that need railway sequences frequently make use of the great variety of locomotives and rolling stock on preserved lines all over Britain. Here, a scene for the James Bond film *Octopussy* is being filmed at the Nene Valley Railway, well known for its collections of European locomotives – in this case a Swedish one.

FOOD AND DRINK

Refreshment rooms are almost as old as the railways themselves. In the early days, before dining cars became commonplace, long-distance trains had scheduled meal stops at major stations such as Swindon, Carlisle and York. These were often as short as ten minutes, so there must have been mayhem at the bars and counters as passengers fought to be served. The food and drink was expensive and not very good – Charles Dickens complained that the soup and the tea tasted the same and the sandwiches were filled with sawdust. Things did improve, however, and by the end of the Victorian era some station restaurants were richly decorated, highly regarded and widely used by the general public as well as railway travellers. Most railway catering was leased to contractors, a pattern maintained until nationalization, when British Railways had its own hotel and restaurant division. This coincided with a move to self-service cafeterias, eventually brought together in 1973 under the Travellers Fare name. After privatization, station catering was thrown wide open to fast-food outlets, famous chains, specialist bars and buffets, and other independent operators. Old-style refreshment rooms have also returned to some smaller stations.

THE GLASGOW CENTRAL

PULLMAN LOUNGE

Let InterCity start your FIRST CLASS JOURNEY before you board the train.

InterCity would like to welcome you to our new Pullman Lounge at Glasgow Central station.

It's the perfect place to relax before your first class trip.

You can catch up with your paperwork, enjoy a complimentary cup of tea or coffee or perhaps phone your office.

The Pullman Lounge also has meeting rooms for up to 10 people for hire which can be booked in advance.

To make use of the Pullman Lounge you must hold a valid first class rail ticket (including Scottish Executive Tickets and first class sleepers) together with a Travel Key, American Express or Pullman Club Card.

◄ There have been many attempts to improve the quality of refreshments, particularly for those prepared to pay premium prices. The Pullman Lounge is a prime example and makes the most of a famous name.

◄ The refreshment pavilion at Lakeside station was justly famous for its setting and views over Windermere and was widely used by the public as well as rail travellers. This promotional postcard was issued by the Furness Railway in the Edwardian era.

◄ Many refreshment rooms were equipped with branded crockery, now collector's items. This Minton cup features the elaborate monogram that was used briefly by the LNER during the 1920s.

LAKE SIDE REFRESHMENT PAVILION.   LAKE SIDE STATION (WINDERMERE).

ON THE CALEDONIAN RAILWAY   WEMYSS BAY TEA ROOM.

▲ Wemyss Bay was a station noted for its setting, its floral displays, its circular booking hall and, not least, its very homely tearoom, featured here on an Edwardian postcard issued by the Caledonian Railway.

◄ Refreshment rooms at stations were regularly updated to reflect contemporary styles. This carefully posed promotional picture shows a recently refurbished room at an unnamed station, redolent with smart Art Deco detailing.

◄ Station catering today is informal. One of many names operating on the platforms is Pumpkin, seen here at Taunton, in the old GWR refreshment room.

FREIGHT AND GOODS

From the very early days railways were built to carry goods or freight and this set a pattern that dominated the structure and principles of the railway system in Britain throughout the 19th century and well into the 20th. The carrying of passengers, initially seen as unimportant or incidental, did begin to dominate railway planning in the 1840s and 1850s and during these decades passenger revenue exceeded the income from goods. From that point the balance shifted, and until the mid-1960s goods revenues were always greater. This was due to a number of factors, including the creation of efficient and nationwide distribution networks, the construction of specialized wagons, the centralization of revenue-gathering via the Railway Clearing House, the development of national parcels services and the improved handling facilities for bulk cargoes. Also significant in the 20th century was the steady integration of road and rail transport systems, to ensure point-to-point collection and delivery, and the use of various kinds of containers to simplify cargo handling.

During the Victorian period many railway fortunes were made, and in some cases subsequently lost, through the great expansion of goods traffic. Notably successful was the carriage of coal, at a time when the country's industrial, commercial and domestic life was entirely dependent upon it, and it was export in prodigious quantities. This pattern was to continue until the early 1950s, when 70 per cent of coal traffic in Britain still went by trai. This resulted in goods trains and goods traffic becoming a familiar feature on practically every line in Britain. Most stations had good

▲ In a scene familiar for over a century, a British Railways classic from the last phase of steam, a class 9F 2-10-0 heavy freight locomotive, no. 92025 of 1955, one of only ten fitted with a Franco-Crosti boiler, hauls a long mixed-goods train across the flat Midlands landscape near Braunston, in 1964.

SOUTHERN RAILWAY.

FROM
TO
Via
(G.W.R) BANBU___ L & N. E. Ry.
(GREAT C___RAL)

Consignee
Date
Wagon No.
Total Sheets in use

◄ With the steam age coming to an end, even the most famous locomotives could find themselves hauling freight trains. In August 1965, a Gresley streamlined A4 Pacific, no. 60027, 'Merlin', makes light work of a cement train near Lunan Bay, south of Montrose.

yards and goods sheds, and even the smallest had some form of freight or parcels-handling facility. In addition, there were many lines, stations and depots built specifically for goods traffic. The majority of railway companies had fleets of goods locomotives, although the realities of railway operation on a day-to-day basis meant that there was a regular crossover between goods and passenger services.

▲ In the summer of 1959 a narrow-profile diesel multiple unit built for the Hastings line overtakes a mixed-goods train near Orpington while the driver of the old Southern Railway N class locomotive, no. 31873, looks on.

▼ The double-headed goods train was always a splendid sight. In the last years of steam some unusual pairings could sometimes be seen, such as an LMS Black 5 and a British Railways 9F, captured here in 1967 fighting the heavy gradients of the Borders with a Whitehaven-to-Gartsherrie goods.

FREIGHT AND GOODS

There were many kinds of goods trains, from the major long-distance services running to regular schedules, to little local pick-up freights collecting the occasional wagon from rural backwaters. However, the most familiar was the mixed freight, a long line of assorted wagons assembled in large marshalling yards and headed by one or two locomotives. Such trains were a regular sight on any railway journey, either rumbling through stations or waiting in sidings and passing loops. Shunting, the process of sorting wagons in major freight yards or rural sidings, was also an integral part of any railway experience, and very familiar to anyone old enough to remember the 1960s and 1970s. The diversity of goods trains, and everything to do with them, was part of their appeal. The modern freight train, usually composed of containers or bulk cargoes such as stone, coal, cement, oil products or new cars, simply cannot compete in terms of character or excitement.

The brake van has also disappeared. Until the 1970s every goods train, however large or small, had to have a brake van, a practice that went back to the 1850s. The brake van was usually a box-like vehicle on four wheels, sometimes with an open verandah, with minimal facilities, such

▲ The mixed freight lived on well into the 1970s and the diesel era. Here, in 1973, assorted wagons topped and tailed by brake vans are hauled past the old Peak Forest station, in Derbyshire, by a class 40 diesel.

► The urban goods train was an important part of the story, even in electrified commuter land. Against the background of a busy yard, a Metropolitan tank hauls a train of empty coal wagons off the Uxbridge branch in the 1930s.

as a stove for the guard, who was in charge of the train. Until the mid-20th century goods wagons often had no linked braking system, so control was dependent upon the locomotive and the guard's handbrake in the brake van. Vacuum braking systems for goods trains were introduced gradually from the 1920s but, even after these were in regular use, the brake van remained an essential part of any goods train. Brake vans varied from company to company but basically they were heavy vehicles, to increase their braking power, and the general design principles remained consistent until the last ones were built in the 1960s. By the 1980s, unbraked or partially-braked goods trains had disappeared and this, combined with the introduction of single-manned or driver-controlled trains, brought the brake van to its end. At the same time, the traditional goods train, a vital component of the railway scene for 150 years, also disappeared from the network.

▲ Steam is in its last year, yet the timeless process of shunting continues. In 1967, amid overgrown sidings at Kirkby Stephen East, a class 4MT locomotive, no. 43049, takes its time while collecting a single open wagon.

▼ In a glorious Cumbrian setting near Lowca in 1968, a Type 1 diesel runs a single brake van along a freight line north of Whitehaven.

GARDENS

The idea of station gardening probably started in the north-east of England but it quickly spread around the country, combining as it did two key principles: fostering pride in the workplace and giving satisfaction to passengers. Many stationmasters were in any case keen gardeners.

Soon, a competitive element was introduced and prizes were offered for the best-kept station and the best station in various categories, initially on a local basis but ultimately regionally and nationally. In 1930 the LNER even fitted a bench to the front of a locomotive to speed up the judging process. Every style of gardening was featured, reflecting the tastes and skills of the station staff, but colourful schemes predominated.

Today some of the best gardens are to be found on preserved lines, but stations on the national network have not given up. Hanging baskets are commonplace and competitions still take place, often encouraged by sponsorship and local tourist boards.

► In the mid-1990s summer colours fill the exuberant beds at Dolau, a halt on the Heart of Wales line. Railways like this, always understaffed and hovering on the edge of survival, rely on local community support.

◄ Raised beds on the platform, often simply made from waste materials and planted with colourful annuals, were always popular, especially if combined with the station name in flowers or painted stones. These were captured at Dulverton, in Devon, in August 1959.

5. ORNAMENTAL ROCK GARDENS, WORLD'S SMALLEST RAILWAY, NEW ROMNEY STATION.

◄ A famous miniature garden on a famous miniature railway: the rock gardens at New Romney, on the Romney, Hythe & Dymchurch in the 1930s, complete with windmill, water features and gnomes.

► Pipe in hand and surrounded by verdant plants, a GWR Inspector poses in front of his rustic pergola, probably in the garden of his house rather than on the station.

▼ Railway gardens were not limited to the platform area or the immediate station surroundings, and sometimes were simply decorative lineside fixtures. Nor were they solely the province of branch and minor lines. Here is a mainline garden, on the old Somerset & Dorset Joint Railway.

HOLIDAYS

The Victorians loved the seaside and it is to them that we owe the enduring pleasures of a day by the sea. It was the railways that made it all possible; indeed, it could be said that the railways made the British seaside. Prior to the railway age, travel to the coast was for most people tedious and expensive, and bathing was more about health than pleasure. From the 1850s it all changed, as the tentacles of the railway system reached more and more stretches of hitherto inaccessible coastline and speculative railway companies opened up lines to the sea in search of increased traffic.

Some established resorts, such as Brighton, Ramsgate and Scarborough, took on a new lease of life when the trains arrived, establishing the idea of the day trip and the seaside excursion. Other places were in effect the creation of the railways, for example Cornwall and the West Country, south Wales, west Wales and north Wales, the Lancashire coast, East Anglia and Lincolnshire, north Yorkshire and Scotland. It was the GWR that first called the south Devon resorts the English Riviera, and similar marketing ploys were dreamed up in railway offices all over the land.

Competition was fierce, and promotion techniques became both intensive and sophisticated. Railways bought or built hotels in favoured resorts, and from the end of the 19th century posters, brochures, handbills and postcards were produced in huge quantities. Everyone remembers John Hassall's 'Skegness is So Bracing' poster, but that was just one of thousands of colourful images that sold to millions the idea of a seaside holiday by train.

Vol.8 No.8 August 1957

British Railways Magazine

London Midland Region

travel in Rail Comfort

◄ The faces say it all: these children interrupt their bucket and spade games to pose for the camera. It is the 1920s and, judging by the sweaters, a bit chilly. The bucket says 'A Present from the Seaside'.

▲ For its August 1957 issue the staff magazine of British Railways London Midland Region featured, unusually for so conventional a publication, a pretty pin-up entitled 'The spirit of the holiday season'.

◀ It is nearly journey's end as a holiday express passes Goodrington Sands en route to Kingswear (for Dartmouth) in May 1959. The prospect of sun, sea and sand stretches ahead.

Driver, Where are you going, Sonny?
Little Boy, "To ____ of course, it is such a jolly place for a holiday."

Photo Reproduced by the courtesy of the Southern Ry.

▲ This famous image was used by the Southern Railway in the 1920s.

◀ It is September 1962 and the holiday is over: a double-headed express from Bournemouth to Nottingham crosses Midford viaduct on the Somerset & Dorset line. Below it are the remains of the Camerton line, used in the filming of *The Titfield Thunderbolt*.

There is no doubt that the railways played a major part in developing the holiday trade. In many parts of Britain, resorts, some of which had been created by railway companies, relied on ever-expanding lists of excursion trains and holiday specials. Several resorts even had separate excursion stations to cater for the weight of traffic.

The interwar years saw the heyday of this business, but in the 1950s, competition from coaches and private cars began to undermine the railway's dominance of the holiday trade.

However, one area did remain faithful to the railway, and that was the holiday camp. Butlin's started to build camps in the 1930s, and their immediate success spawned dozens more all around the coast of Britain. Sites were chosen because of their good railway access and in many places, for example Pwllheli, in Wales, and Filey, in Yorkshire, special holiday camp stations were built. By the 1970s, while holiday camps continued to flourish, they were no longer dependent upon the railway.

PRESTATYN HOLIDAY CAMP

The Chalet Village by the Sea

ENQUIRIES AND RESERVATIONS at any LMS Station or Office of Thos. Cook & Son Ltd.   TRAVEL BY LMS

◀ In July 1957, hauled by a powerful old LNER K3 locomotive, a long holiday camp special sets off from Lowestoft filled with, one hopes, happy campers on their way home. Such specials were a regular feature of many summer timetables.

◄ In the 1930s, holiday camps enjoyed a smart, contemporary image and their publicity, often arranged jointly with a railway company, underlined this. Typical of this is this LMS poster promoting Prestatyn Holiday Camp in north Wales, which was close to the railway.

► One of the holiday camps with its own dedicated station was Filey, on the Yorkshire coast, in this case at the end of a short branch line. Long platforms and storage sidings catered for the huge holiday specials that were still running in 1965, when this photograph was taken. It was March, so there were few passengers. Most of them seem to be looking at the old LNER locomotive.

BUTLIN'S SKEGNESS
Monorail

▲ During the 1960s holiday camps continued to develop, broadening their appeal and the range of their facilities. This postcard shows the monorail that Butlin's installed at their Skegness camp, as a novelty rather than as a practical means of transport. Ironically, although Skegness was railway connected, few of its clients were by this time travelling to or from the camp by the real train.

Seaside holidays in pre-World War I Britain were about sea, sun and fun. This jolly family is having a good time, perhaps at a resort on the Yorkshire coast. At traditional resorts such as Scarborough, bathing machines remained in use throughout this period.

"View of the Sea from the Promenade!"

◄ No seaside holiday was complete until a saucy postcard had been sent back home. This 1930s classic by Donald McGill was posted in Bournemouth, with an equally classic message: 'Comfortable ride down. Very nice digs. Lovely weather. Everything OK.'

HOTELS

Railways and hotels grew up alongside each other and were mutually interdependent. The first hotel built by a railway company opened at Euston in London in 1839, and from this point the acquisition, building and management of hotels became a significant part of railway business. Eventually all London termini with the exception of Fenchurch Street, Blackfriars and, surprisingly, Waterloo boasted a hotel, while equally impressive structures were to be found in Birmingham, Manchester, Liverpool, Leeds, Glasgow, Edinburgh and elsewhere. In some large cities served by several railway companies there were competing hotels. Major architects were involved, for example EM Barry at Charing Cross in London, Alfred Waterhouse at the North Western in Liverpool and George Gilbert Scott at St Pancras. Scott's Midland Grand Hotel is now one of the landmarks of London and its Gothic splendour is widely seen as the epitome of railway age architecture.

Although associated primarily with major towns and cities, railway hotels were soon to be found in ports, notably at Holyhead, Dover and Parkeston Quay, and provincial towns. Later, with the spread of leisure travel, railway hotels took their place in the development of seaside, sporting and country resorts. One of the earliest seaside hotels was the Zetland, built by the Stockton & Darlington at the developing resort of Saltburn. Later, railway-owned golf hotels became popular, especially in Scotland, with famous examples at Turnberry, Gleneagles and Cruden Bay. At first conservative and restrained in style, hotel architecture became more flamboyant and extravagant as the century progressed and as the ambitions, power and wealth of railway companies increased.

◀ Hull's Royal Station Hotel, completed in 1851, was one of the first to be built across the station concourse facing the platforms, a layout that soon became standard. British Transport Hotels was formed in 1962 to manage the remaining 37 railway hotels, and it survived until the early 1980s, when everything was privatized. This brochure dates from the 1970s.

▲ The LNWR's Queens Hotel at Birmingham New Street was opened in 1854. Built in a formal classical style, it echoed the architecture favoured by the North Western's predecessor, the London & Birmingham, creators of London's Euston and Birmingham's Curzon Street stations.

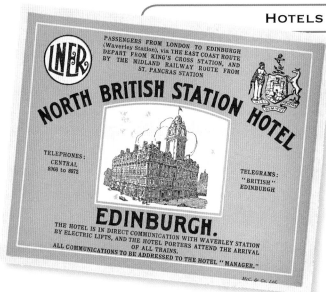

▲ The Glasgow & South Western was an adventurous company with interests in coal and tourism. It owned a number of hotels, including the famous golf hotel at Turnberry, and promoted them in an attractive way.

▲ The North British Railway opened its grand hotel overlooking Edinburgh's Waverley station in 1902. The massive ten-storey stone structure was dominated by its great clock tower, one of Edinburgh's best-loved landmarks. This label, a typical railway hotel souvenir, dates from the LNER era.

▼ The Wyncliff Hotel, originally a private house, was acquired by the Great Western in 1898. Renamed The Fishguard Bay, it was extensively enlarged to serve the Irish trade in 1906. This card, dating from that period, shows its woodland setting away from the railway.

FURNESS ABBEY HOTEL.   FURNESS ABBEY STATION.

THE FISHGUARD BAY HOTEL.   Under the management of the Great Western Railway Co

▲ The prosperity of the Furness Railway in Cumbria was closely associated with the steel industry. When this trade declined in the 1880s, the railway switched to the promotion of tourism and enjoyed a new lease of life. The country-house style Furness Abbey Hotel dates from this period.

Midland Hotel, Manchester.
Roof Garden.

▲ Although a relatively late arrival on the scene, in 1903, Manchester's Midland Hotel was one of the most spectacular. Its facilities included an 800-seat theatre and the roof garden shown on this card.

The heyday of the railway hotel was probably at the end of the Victorian era, and in 1901 there were 61. In the 1920s and 1930s some hotels were closed but others were renovated in a smart Art Deco style. Best known of these was the widely promoted and highly fashionable Midland at Morecambe, designed by Oliver Hill in 1930. The hotels were separated from railway ownership in 1948 but came back under railway control in 1962 as British Transport Hotels, only to be sold completely in the early 1980s.

In architectural terms the railway hotel was the perfect reflection of Victorian

attract custom. Huge and impressive dining rooms, lounges and public spaces were regula[r] renovated in the latest styles, while equally important were special features such as theatr[e] conference rooms and gardens. A remarkable example of this was the roof garden on top of the Midland Hotel in Manchester, which offered fine views across the city – weather permitting. Indeed, the Midland was famous for its hotels, the best known being the Gran[d] at London's St Pancras station, which opened [in] 1873. Closure at an early date and subsequen[t]

YORK, ROYAL STATION HOTEL : THE LOUNGE

◄ York's Royal Station Hotel was opened in 1878. Extended in 1896, it had been lavishly refitted by the time this card was issued in about 1914. By then it boasted electric lights, an electric lift, a motor garage, a typewriting room and 'one of the handsomest reading rooms in the kingdom'.

ambition and extravagance. Classical, Gothic, Renaissance and French styles were favoured for the exteriors, and these were generally echoed by the interiors, which became more lavish as the century progressed. With their combinations of modern facilities and exciting decor and fittings, these hotels existed in a highly competitive environment, vying to

use as offices enabled the original interiors to survive. Now being fully restored, these offer a unique insight into the glorious and rich extravagance of the Victorian railway hotel. At the end of the 19th century styles became more informal, with echoes of Arts & Crafts and Art Nouveau, and then in the 1920s and 1930s came modernism and Art Deco.

North Western Hotel, Liverpool. — New Grill Room, open to non-residents.

▲ Liverpool's first railway hotel was the North Western and its dominant position remained unchallenged until the Midland railway took over and extensively rebuilt the Adelphi in the Edwardian era. This prompted a major updating of the North Western by the LNWR, illustrated in this card.

The Midland Grand at London St Pancras, designed by Gilbert Scott and opened in 1873, was the greatest and most lavish railway hotel in Britain. Today, its spiky Gothic exterior is the icon of the railway age. More remarkable is the survival of its glorious interior, now restored.

▲ The glorious stone vaulted ceiling above the grand staircase of the Midland Grand at London St Pancras.

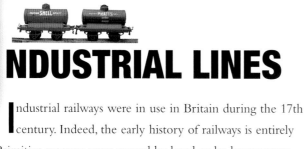

NDUSTRIAL LINES

Industrial railways were in use in Britain during the 17th century. Indeed, the early history of railways is entirely industrial. Primitive wagons were moved by hand or by horsepower on wooden, stone or cast-iron tramways through much of the 18th and early 19th centuries, serving collieries, quarries and iron works. Gauges and sizes varied hugely, from under 2ft to 7ft. Such railways were limited in scale and generally isolated. It was not until a national railway network began to emerge that there was any attempt at standardization or any need to construct sidings that could connect with standard-gauge lines.

▲ Some industrial locomotives were clearly descended from traction engines and road rollers and some makers, such as Aveling Barford, did produce both. This typically hybrid example was owned by the Cement Marketing Board – hence its name, 'The Blue Circle'.

▼ Many systems were self-contained but others were linked to the main line, with industrial locomotives being used to take wagons to and from the factory sidings.

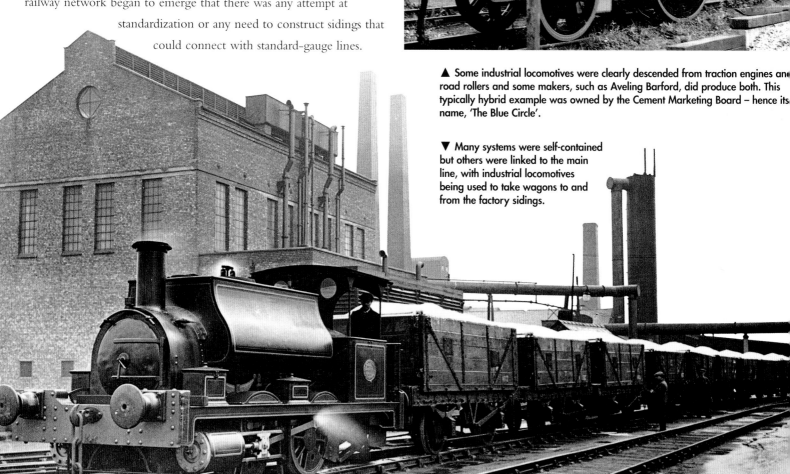

◀ The diversity of industrial locomotives was extraordinary, with many apparently bearing the stamp of Heath Robinson. This eccentric chain-driven example carries a nameplate, 'Allen Lambert', a common practice with such locomotives and reflective of the pride of their operators and their frequent longevity in service.

The earliest steam locomotives, by Trevithick, Blenkinsop and George Stephenson, were built for industrial use. These were followed by a hotchpotch of secondhand and one-off engines that became the mainstay of industrial lines for decades. It was not until the 1860s that manufacturers such as Manning Wardle began to produce ranges of small locomotives specifically for industrial railways, and production in one form or another has continued to the present day.

The diversity of industrial railways in regard to their locomotives, rolling stock and fields of activity was always part of their appeal. Coal was the major user, but to that could be added quarries for stone, slate, sand, clay, iron ore and gravel, as well as brick works, chemical works, breweries, shipyards,

▶ Quarry locomotives by Manning Wardle, Hawthorn and others were built for use on irregular and often temporary narrow-gauge track, usually 3ft or less. These three, long out of use, await the cutter's torch.

◀ Looking smart, despite its age, and posing proudly with its crew, 'Covertcoat' is a typical Leeds-built quarry locomotive of 1898. A rare survivor, this now has a very different life on the Launceston Railway.

67

docks and corporate activities such as gas and water works, power-generating plants and industrial estates. There was considerable use in agriculture and forestry, particularly for the bulk transport of sugar beet, potatoes and peat. Contractors have always used industrial railways on construction projects, many of which were by definition short-lived, so some manufacturers produced easily transportable vehicles and tracks designed for temporary use. Associated with these was the development of locomotives driven by petrol or diesel engines. In some cases contractors who built early railways ended up running them themselves, using whatever locomotives and rolling stock that could be found. However, passenger-carrying was never a real concern, though some lines had carriages suitable for transporting people to and from work. Industrial lines have declined massively since the 1960s, but a recent example was the extensive network, with over a hundred locomotives, used for some years during the building of the Channel Tunnel.

▲ This smartly turned-out Andrew Barclay 0-4-0 worked at one of ICI's chemical plants. Industrial locomotives were often very well cared for and many enjoyed a long life, with one or a number of owners.

▼ Some industrial locomotives enjoyed a remarkably long life. This Hawthorn 0-4-0 was approaching its centenary when photographed still in use in 1950 at a pottery works. Clay and industrial ceramics businesses, such as brick and pipe works, were major users of industrial railways.

▲ Many gas works had narrow-gauge railways which often featured low-profile locomotives designed to move easily among the retort sheds. No. 13 is seen here at work at Beckton, in east London, in 1954.

▲ The combined challenge of road transport and industrial decline was too much for many industrial railways and from the 1960s, thousands of locomotives went to the scrapyard.

▲ Until its devastation in the 1980s, the coal industry was the mainstay of the railways. Collieries had their own railway networks, operated by aged industrial tank locomotives. Steam survived long after it had gone from British Railways. Here, in 1979, 'Warrior', an ex-War Department locomotive, struggles to haul a rake of loaded wagons away from Bickershaw Colliery, Leigh, near Manchester.

▶ Many industries had their own railway networks and their own vehicles. Typical was the brewing industry, which depended on the railway for supplies of raw materials and the transport of the beer. At the Bass brewery in Burton-on-Trent, one of its own locomotives collects wagons from the main line in 1958.

IRONWORK

Architectural cast iron is one of the wonders of the Victorian era and it was the adventurous use of this material, for stations, bridges and other structures, that was the practical foundation of the railway age. Cast iron was first used as a building material in the 18th century, but it really came of age from the 1830s. Great strength and stability, combined with rich decorative detail, made it the perfect material for the vast trainshed roofs of the early stations, such as Paddington or York. However,

▲ Cast-iron spandrels and canopy supports were ideal for the decorative display of railway company initials and monograms. Many survive to be enjoyed today. This is the Taff Vale Railway's monogram at Porth station.

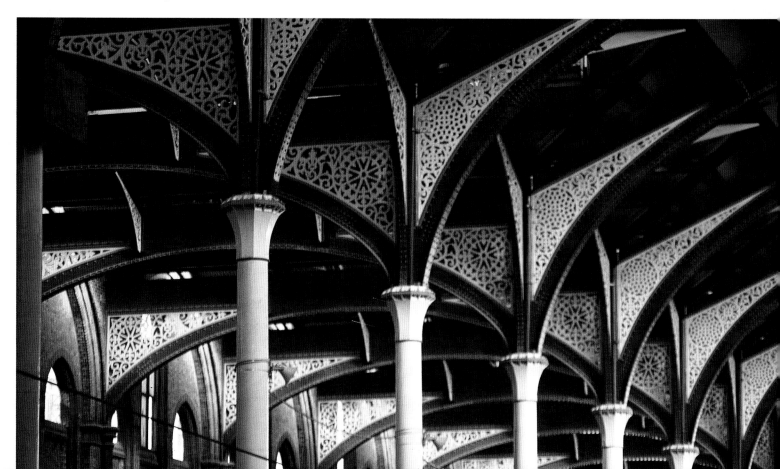

◀ Built originally to mark a junction, Hellifield gradually became the centre of a substantial railway community. The present station, dating from 1880, is notable for its decorative cast ironwork.

was equally suitable for many other ses, including canopy supports, signal d lighting posts, fences, gates, benches d notices. For bridges and other load-earing and flexible structures it was oon replaced by wrought iron, but in l other areas cast iron remained king. hus, decorative cast iron is one of the ost distinctive products of the railway ge. Its legacy is still to be enjoyed all ver Britain.

Cast- and wrought-iron fencing outside arylebone station features the initials of the reat Central Railway, the station's builders, who ompleted this, London's last terminus, in 1899.

◀ The great iron train sheds combined great ructural strength with delicate cast detail nd rich colours. This is Liverpool Street, in ondon, built in 1875 and sensitively restored the 1990s.

▲ A vast, once-busy station dating originally from 1847, Tynemouth is now served by the Tyne and Wear metro system. It was rebuilt in 1882 when the acres of cast-iron-supported canopies were added.

JOKES

The comic postcard and the seaside holiday are inseparable parts of the British cultural experience. They grew up together, sharing a love of vulgarity and innuendo that goes right to the heart of the British character. The themes are predictable and universal and, remarkably, in these days of political correctness they all survive – as a glance at the postcard racks in any seaside resort will show. Favourite topics include marriage and domestic incompatibility, drunkenness and excess, obesity and sexism. Among the most popular settings are the beach, the hotel, the office or place of work, and the railway, the latter because of the direct link between railways and holidays.

There are hundreds of comic railway cards, most of which follow certain themes: slow trains and delays on the line, discomfort and overcrowding, misunderstood announcements by railway staff and places with unpronounceable names (usually in Wales), romance, marriage and sex, women travelling alone, the class system and drunken passengers. Variations on these themes can be found throughout the history of the comic railway card, from about 1904 right up to the present day, an indication that certain aspects of the British character are unchangeable.

"IT'S NOT THE SIGNALS—IT'S THE WIND THAT'S AGAINST US!"

"SHAY GUARD, DOES THISH TRA CLAP AT STOPHAM JUNCTION"

This is something like we came to Blackpool
OWING TO THE SCARCITY OF TRAINS.

These three cards illustrate three favourite railway themes: misunderstandings between staff and passengers, delay and discomfort, and drunken passengers. They cover a wide range of dates, from the 1950s at the top, 1927 to the right and 1917 below (with the message having a reference to the war). They all say 'having a fine time, weather good!'.

NEW PORTER: "IF THERE'S ANYONE 'ERE FOR THERE 'ERE IT IS!"

LLANFAIRPWLLGWYNCYLLGOCERYCH...

"ALL CHANGE!"
"I'VE CHANGED EVERYTHING BUT MY CHEMISE, GUARD. HAVE I TO CHANGE THAT AN' ALL?"

These cards explore the popular theme of misunderstandings between staff and passengers. The station with the longest name, in Anglesey, usually called LlanfairPG for short, has inspired several cards, above left being a 1950s example. The postcard to the right, from 1911, features the marital theme with a ponderous pun (sadly, there never was a station called Sawyer). Confusion about changing trains is a familiar theme, represented in this 1927 card above right. Earliest, from 1904 and used as a birthday card, is the drunken ticket office exchange to the left.

FELLOW TRAVELLERS

"Hic, gimme a ticket pleash,"
"Very well" said the clerk "where do you wish to go!"
"You mindsh yer own buishness" says he,
"And gimme a ticket, and no pertinence,
I've got the money to pay, stand on me,"
Then the clerk gets annoyed, and says "hurry up, please,
What station do you want, don't talk rot,"
"What stationsh I want, why, I never thought of that,
I dunno, what stationsh have yer got?"

482

"SAWYER! SAWYER!!"
"ORL RIGHT, WE DON'T CARE IF YOU DID, WE WERE MARRIED THIS MORNING!"

KIDS

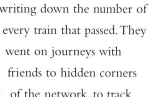

Children and trains are inseparable. Generations have been brought up on train books, notably the Thomas the Tank Engine series, and toy trains. Children are fascinated by trains, they watch them, they like the noise and the atmosphere, and even modern children seem to understand the appeal of steam. In the past, trains were central to children's lives. Children went to school by train, on holiday by train, to the shops, cinemas and coffee bars by train. Many became train fanatics, standing in groups or on their own on busy platforms, efficiently writing down the number of every train that passed. They went on journeys with friends to hidden corners of the network, to track

▲ In a scene now impossible in the age of CCTV, two small boys sit the platform edge in Leeds in July 1977 to have a good look at the bi Deltic locomotive across the track

▼ Immersed in their own world, three schoolgirls chatter their way along the platform at Dymock station, on the Gloucester to Ledbury line, in July 1959, without a thought for the unusual 1930s GWR railcar that has brought them there.

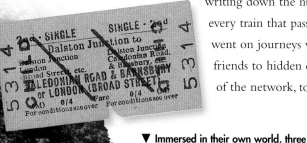

▲ Three classic young rail enthusiasts pose for a friend's camera on the platform at Burghclere station, in Berkshire, in the 1950s. They can take their time, for the station is deserted and the line from Newbury to Winchester Chesil was never very busy.

▲ The celebrations for the 150th anniversary of the ...aff Vale Railway were held at Merthyr Tydfil station ...n 12 April 1991. Smart locomotives attended and ...local school orchestra played on the platform.

...own elderly branch lines and ancient ...ocomotives long past retirement. They ...ravelled on children's tickets, half-price to ...he age of 14, and then it was all over. They ...eft school and started work or went to ...ollege; now it was the real world and the ...rains became a means of getting from A to B. ...s adults, they did their courting by train, but ...hat is another story…

It is early September in 1961 and there is plenty of ...ctivity on the platforms at Taunton, in Somerset. Some ...irl Guides, unsmiling, are on their way home from ...ummer camp, two small boys run about in front of ...he photographer, and on the locomotive the fireman ...ans out of the cab window, looking the other way and ...aiting for something to happen.

LINESIDE FEATURES

Something that used to enliven the journeys of keen-eyed passengers was the amazing number and variety of signs and bits of equipment there used to be alongside the line. Most obvious were the signals and the signalling infrastructure, along with the machinery that made the railways operate properly and safely, such as point levers. However, there was very much more than this, all of it integral to the railway scene across the network but now lost for ever. The list included mileposts, gradient posts, bridge plates and boundary markers, all of which reflected the concern for precision, detail and order that characterized the railway age. Equally impressive was the variety of signs. Made of wood, concrete, cast iron and enamel, most were warnings or admonitions, often written in forms of English that now seem archaic and pedantic. In the Victorian and Edwardian eras, each railway company had its own style and colours, adding greatly to the diversity of these signs; many were still in use decades after the formation of the Big Four in 1923.

Aside from signs, there were also the more significant lineside structures: the platelayers' huts, the water

▶ Most signs were factory-made to well-defined styles and specifications, but the trackside was also littered with 'home-made' examples, often produced in local workshops. Many were delightfully eccentric, like this one near Liskeard, Cornwall.

▶ ▶ In the past even the smallest station had sidings, and the sets of points that accessed these were controlled by hand-operated levers of the kind shown here. Some survive around the network but these are relatively rare.

▼ Lineside mileposts, marking each quarter, half and full mile, were a feature of early railways and were made compulsory by an Act of 1845. Made in wood, iron and, later, concrete, these varied in style – as indicated on this 1950s GWR postcard.

4-6-0 No. 1023 'County of Oxford' County Class. Great Western Railway. Driving wheels 6' 3". Two cylinders 18½" diam. x 30" stroke. Boiler pressure 250 lb/in². Tractive effort 29,050 lb.

◀ Steam locomotives need constant supplies of water. In the 1860s an automatic means of refilling the tender was developed, whereby a scoop lowered by the fireman collected water from long troughs laid between the tracks. Here, a Britannia class 4-6-2, no. 70020 'Mercury', passes over Bushey troughs, in Hertfordshire, with a fitted freight.

▶ Victorian concern for detail ensured that railway companies marked the limits of their territory. Fencing was the most common marker, but also used were cast-iron boundary posts bearing the company's initials, in this case those of the Mid Wales Railway.

▼ Changes in ownership often gave rise to groups of lineside signs, especially of the type giving warnings to the public. Here, near Betchworth, Surrey, there were two signs in cast iron, from L&SWR and SE&CR, a battered enamel one from the Southern and a delightfully worded but clearly handmade wooden one from British Railways.

towers, the loading gauges and the water troughs between the tracks. Then there were the thousands of miles of telegraph and telephone wires looping along between the wooden posts that lined even the most minor railway; each wire was connected to a ceramic insulator, which was frequently stamped with the initials of the railway company that owned the line. The corporate image, or house style, was of great importance, and often a matter of pride to the railway companies, and trackside equipment was just as vital a component of that image as the stations and the trains. Even the most minor things carried the company name or monogram and those that survive naturally appeal to both the historian and the collector.

▲ The platelayers' hut was a common lineside feature and quite a number have lived on long after closure of the line they served. This one is on the M&GN network in Norfolk.

▲ Cast-iron boundary markers, generally being small and unobtrusive, often get overlooked and left behind by the salvage gangs following line closures. This North Eastern example survives at Lartington, near Barnard Castle.

◄ Old iron signs littered the network until the 1980s, but survivors in situ are now rare. This example is in a hedge near Wisbech.

▲ All railway companies were concerned about trespassers, so notices threatening prosecution were put up with great frequency. Usually made in cast iron, these varied widely in style, size and message from company to company. Such notices are not uncommon today but their appeal to the collector is dependent upon their rarity. A dual-language one like this, issued by a minor company, the Brecon & Merthyr Railway, would be far more appealing than a standard GWR example.

◄ Station nameboards came in many shapes and styles, in wood, metal, enamel, concrete and even plastic. Legibility was the aim, and some companies favoured raised lettering, believing the shadow would make it show up better. Great care was taken with punctuation.

▲ A delightful and common statement of individuality was the marking of station names in unusual ways. White-painted stones set into gravel or grass, were popular, but grand stations justified grander schemes, as in this fine example from York.

▼ Some trespass notices can be dated by the names included in the message, such as this NER example, now preserved and attached to the wall of a former station in the Whitby area, North Yorkshire.

NORTH EASTERN RAILWAY PUBLIC WARNING
PERSONS ARE WARNED NOT TO TRESPASS ON THIS RAILWAY, OR ON ANY OF THE LINES, STATIONS, WORKS, OR PREMISES CONNECTED THEREWITH.
ANY PERSON SO TRESPASSING IS LIABLE TO A PENALTY OF FORTY SHILLINGS.
C. N. WILKINSON
SECRETARY.

▼ The comprehension of important information was often hindered by a complex and archaic use of English. British Railways seemed to make a point of this, as this crossing warning sign demonstrates.

Maker's plates were to be found on many things, from locomotives and wagons to station girders, signal posts and bridges. This example is on a bridge near Masbury, on the former Somerset & Dorset line.

B.R. NOTICE
PASSENGERS ARE REQUESTED NOT TO CROSS THE LINE, UNTIL THE TRAIN HAS DEPARTED SO THEY MAY AVOID DANGER IN CASE TRAIN MAY BE APPROACHING ON THE OPPOSITE SIDE.   BY ORDER.

LOST RAILWAY COMPANIES

The railway network of Britain was constructed in a piecemeal way by hundreds of independent companies, mainly during the Victorian era. Some were set up to build major trunk routes linking the industrial and population centres of Britain, while others were entirely local affairs, raising money to construct the few miles of track that would link their town or village to the main network. Whatever their size or ambition, all were united by their belief in the social and economic power of the railway. Some were successful, others failed. Some small ones were short-lived, and were soon swallowed up by their larger neighbours.

By the end of the 19th century the major companies dominated the network, but many minor ones retained their independence until the 1923 Grouping, when the vast majority were absorbed into the Big Four – GWR, SR, LMS and LNER. The greatest survival from the years of independence is paperwork. Every company, however small, had its own look, its own style and its own paperwork. These documents, still surprisingly accessible to collectors, are a memorial to railway diversity.

▶ The original main line of the North British Railway from Berwick to Edinburgh opened in 1846. It expanded steadily by taking over other companies and, by the time it was absorbed into the LNER, its network included over 50 railways. In 1878 it opened the notorious Tay bridge.

▲ The Bristol & Exeter was an early broad-gauge line completed in 1844. By absorbing other companies, it eventually operated a network of more than 200 miles. It was taken over itself by the GWR in 1876, having already been converted to standard gauge.

◀ The Brecon & Merthyr Tydfil Junction Railway was authorized between 1859 and 1862, and its route was completed in 1868. It remained independent until 1922, when it was absorbed into the GWR. Its route, closed in 1964, contained the highest tunnel in Britain, at 1312ft.

INWARD GOODS.

No. 4

DUNDEE AND ARBROATH JOINT RAILWAY.—Goods Department.

STATION, 12/6/9?

have Carted out from the Station, for delivery,

| Tons. | Cwts. | Qrs. | Lbs. | Consigned to |

Weighing......

: 5 :

For which Cartage is charged by the Railway Company.

Number of Smalls, Empties,

Carter. Weigher.

◄ The Dundee & Arbroath was opened in 1840, built to a 5ft 6in gauge, and it remained isolated until 1848. Later, in 1880, it became part of the Caledonian and North British networks.

► The South Eastern, one of the major railways in south-eastern England, completed its line to Dover in 1844. The famous works at Ashford was built a few years later. From 1899 it operated jointly with its rival, the London, Chatham & Dover, becoming the South Eastern & Chatham.

South Eastern and Chatham Railway.

Reading Station. No. 200565

EXCESS FARE RECEIPT. 27 day of July 1912

From Guilaford to Reading

No. of Passengers.

1S.	2S.	3S.	1R.	2R.	3R.	Particulars of Excess.	Amount.
	2					No. Ticket	s. 5 d. 6
						Ticket out of Date	
						Cheap to Ordinary	
						Over Distance ...	
						Child over Age ...	
						2nd to 1st ...	
						3rd to 1st ...	
						3rd to 2nd ...	

Train 2/35 No. of Ticket excessed

Signature.

Issued subject to the Committee's published and Regulations.

LANCASTER AND CARLISLE RAILWAY.

CASTLE STATION, LANCASTER, Nov. 1853.

CAUTION TO BREAKSMEN.

Every breaksman in charge of a train, shall before starting, carefully examine the break of his van, to see that it is in good order, well oiled, and that all the pins and cotters are properly secured. Any breaksman neglecting this order will be fined

South Western & Midland Railway Companies'
Somerset & Dorset Joint Line.

(492)

INSURED.

(No.)

From

in

Date

187

◄ The Somerset & Dorset Railway completed its line in 1874 but financial problems meant that it was operated from 1875 jointly by the LSWR and the Midland.

▲ The Lancaster & Carlisle's expensive and demanding route was completed in 1846 but it soon became part of the LNWR's west coast main line from London to Scotland.

'To be used only for Traffic at the Newspaper scale, the No. of Parcels not to be counted in abstracting)

MARYPORT & CARLISLE RAILWAY.
COCKERMOUTH to

(R.A.—1902). Guards' Signatures :—

Via

NEWSPAPER PARCELS WAY BILL.

Departure o'clock Train day of 19

No.	Name.	Destination.	Weight. lbs.	Value of Labels. s. d.	TO PAY. £ s. d.	TRAFFIC NOT LABELLED. PAID. £ s. d.	Sender
1	Ridley		6				
2							
3							
4							
5							

N.B.—The Guard of the Train must see that the Entries on this Bill correspond with the Parcels delivered to and given up by him.

► After a lengthy and tortuous gestation, the Maryport & Carlisle opened its 28-mile route in 1845. It then managed to remain independent until 1923.

MAIL AND PARCELS

By an 1838 Act of Parliament the Postmaster General was empowered to require any railway company to carry the mail. The same year saw the introduction of the first travelling post offices, mobile sorting offices initially converted from horse boxes. The service grew rapidly. By the 1850s dedicated mail trains were in use and from 1882 post boxes were fitted to mail trains. Parcel post was carried by train from the early 1880s. By the 1860s the automatic exchange of mailbags between the trackside and a moving train had been perfected, and by 1911 there were 245 locations where this could take place. By 1967 only 34 remained, and the system was last used in 1971. The layout of the vehicles, with sorting boxes on one side and hooks for mail bags on the other, changed little during the life of the travelling post offices (TPOs). In recent times, with more mail and parcels going by road, the number of TPOs began to diminish. In the early 1990s London was still handling 68 trains a day, but there was then a rapid decline and the mail trains stopped in 2004 only to restart in a limited way a few years later.

In 1967 some mail trains were still steam-hauled, including this one, heading north near Tebay on the West Coast main line. The water troughs, for automatically filling the tanks in the locomotive's tender, are still in place between the tracks.

This LNWR official postcard from the Edwardian era shows the company's latest travelling post office, complete with apparatus for collecting and discharging mail bags at speed.

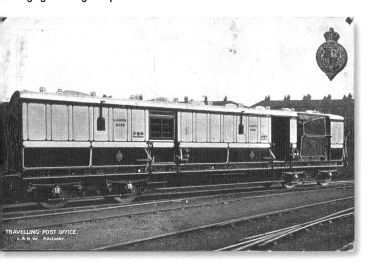

TRAVELLING-POST-OFFICE.
L.&N.W. RAILWAY.

▲ 'Postmen of the British Empire' was the title of a series of postcards issued in 1904 depicting postal services around the empire. This one shows mail bags being loaded prior to the departure of the Night Mail from some British city. Mail was carried on many passenger trains, as well as on the dedicated mail trains and travelling post offices.

◀ Mail bags piled up on trolleys on the platform and awaiting the train used to be a common sight at stations all over Britain, but this is now a distant memory. Pictured here, in 1964, is Glastonbury Street station, where the mail bags would have been loaded onto the train for Evercreech Junction for onward transport to a regional sorting office or TPO.

SHREWSBURY 2 NOV 1981
SHREWSBURY–YORK T.P.O.

◀ ▲ The process of sorting the mail on a TPO did not change from its inception in early Victorian days until the last regular services were withdrawn in 2004. This shows the sorters on the regular Shrewsbury to York service. Above is an example of the special TPO postmark, used on letters posted in the box that was attached to the carriage.

MAINTENANCE

Steam locomotives were demanding machines, requiring constant attention. Apart from regular coaling, watering and ash removal, there was a continual round of oiling, greasing and adjustment to be carried out on shed, in the sidings or yards, or at station stops. Quality of performance was related directly to maintenance, so both driver and fireman were always busy. Their jobs required a unique combination of experience, instinct, anticipation and dedication, but for all that it was a highly regulated industry, with rules and rule books to cover most eventualities. Driver and fireman were in charge of their locomotive while it was in their care but the more major maintenance work was carried out by the engineers attached to the sheds. This could range from day-to-day maintenance to major repairs and overhauls. While coaling and ash removal were usually shed activities, water was a constant requirement, so water columns and towers were universal in the steam age, and every station of any stature would have at least one. Rolling stock, signalling equipment and the track itself were also subject to scheduled maintenance programmes.

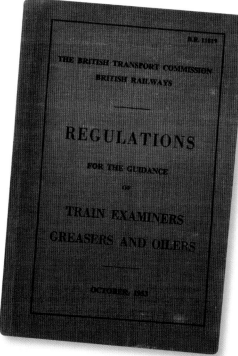

▲ In the railway world there were rules and regulations about everything, and the smooth operation of the network was entirely dependent upon their being strictly adhered to.

◄ An old Drummond 0-6-0 Jumbo takes on water at Motherwell in the 1950s while the crew enjoy a short breather. With care and good maintenance, an ancient locomotive could work for decades.

► A serious discussion, apparently about oiling, takes place between the driver and fireman of class A1 locomotive 60143 'Sir Walter Scott' at Newcastle shed while the wheel-tapper looks on.

◄ LNER class B1 'Topi' receives some minor attention at the end of the Meltham branch, near the junction with the Huddersfield-to-Penistone line, which lies beyond the signal box.

◄ ▲ Aspects of locomotive maintenance, on shed and on the road, are captured in photographs taken at Newcastle in the 1950s. These range from setting the head code (top left) to cleaning out the tubes, which was always a thankless and unpopular job (left).

▼ Water towers, of constantly varied form, were positioned at regular intervals throughout the network. Here, in June 1960, GWR Prairie tank no. 4557 takes water at Glogue Halt, while the passengers in the 4.00pm Whitland-to-Cardigan train enjoy the sunshine through the windows.

► Locomotives on branchline duties might be away from the main shed for days on end, so regular maintenance was down to the crew. This was usually carried out at the line's terminus, where limited facilities were available. At Lyme Regis in Dorset, in August 1945, the fireman from Adams radial tank no. 520 gets down to the task of removing cinders from the smokebox.

▲ Track maintenance was also demanding. Here, at Eridge, near Tunbridge Wells, in 1932, water is taken into the old tenders used for weed killing along the line, while interested spectators look on.

► A smart Stanier Black Five stands by the coaling tower at Kentish Town shed, in north London, on a sunny day in 1958, while an equally smart, and very lucky, trainspotter has made sure that his friend records the moment.

MILITARY

The first military railway was built inside Woolwich Arsenal, the second at Chatham dockyard. From the 1860s networks, both narrow and standard gauge, serving naval dockyards and ordnance depots spread quickly. Some were massive networks. By 1918 Woolwich Arsenal had 120 miles of railway. The rapid expansion of the army volunteer corps from that period also influenced the development of military railways, though for some time regular trains were used for transport to and from the camps, which tended in any case to be temporary. It was in the 1900s, in the build-up towards World War I, that many permanent camps were established, mostly in Surrey, Hampshire and Wiltshire, notably around Salisbury Plain. Increasingly, these were served by dedicated branch lines with their own stations and infrastructure.

TIDWORTH BARRACKS, SALISBURY PLAIN.

▲ This Edwardian postcard shows the massive military installation at Tidworth, Wiltshire. Beyond the pony and trap, the station, which opened in 1901, is spread across the middle ground, with the camp beyond.

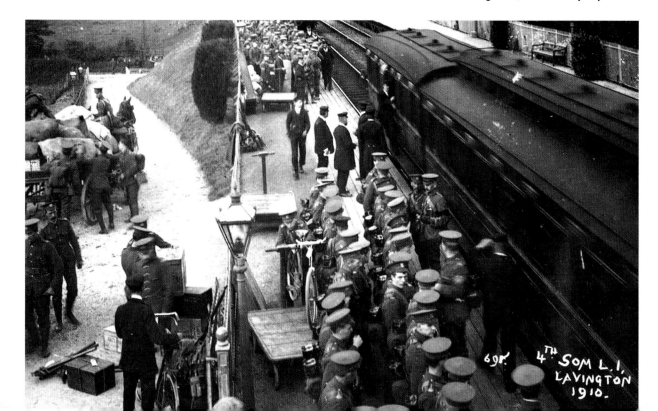

◄ Until World War I many army camps relied on regular stations and trains for their troop movements. Here, in 1910, the 4th Somerset Light Infantry form up on the platform at Lavington, a GWR mainline station east of Westbury, in Wiltshire, on their way to summer camp.

69P. 4TH SOM L.I. LAVINGTON 1910.

The list was substantial by 1914 and included Bisley, Bordon, Bulford, Longmoor, Lydd and Tidworth. Many others were added during World War I, including now famous names such as Blandford, Catterick and Pirbright. Still more followed in World War II. In most cases there was a military station at the end of a siding or branch, but sometimes there were complete military networks with several stations, notably Catterick and Longmoor. The latter had 13 stations on its line from Bentley to Liss. At various times there were

▲ Until it closed in 1969 the Longmoor Military Railway was famous for its open days. Here, in the late 1960s, crowds watch the railway's star, the now preserved 2-10-0 War Department locomotive 'Gordon'.

Booking Hall Nº 2.
Deepcut Camp Station.

London and South Western Ry.
787
FROM WATERLOO TO
BISLEY CAMP

◄ Bisley, in Surrey, was one of the first military stations when it opened in 1890. Later, the branch that served it was extended to Pirbright, Deepcut and Blackdown. This postcard shows the 'other ranks' booking hall at Deepcut Camp station, complete with news-stand.

► Troops parade at Ludgershall, Wiltshire, a public station on the Midland & South Western Junction line north from Andover. However, it had massive sidings and special platforms for military use, and a branch went from here to Tidworth. Today, Ludgershall is a military stores depot, so the line from Andover remains open to serve it, although everything to the north was closed in the 1960s, including the Tidworth branch.

at least 60 dedicated stations serving army camps, and many others serving naval bases, ordnance depots and military hospitals. There were also navy and air force railways with their own stations. Some navy railways were in dockyard complexes such as Devonport and Rosyth; others were distinct branch lines, for example those serving Cairnryan, Faslane and Shoeburyness. As for the air force, Cranwell and Manston had their own branch lines, while other airfields, including Finningley, had their own stations. Most military stations disappeared after World War II. Few survive, apart from stores depots such as Bicester and Ludgershall.

▲ Set up in 1905, the Longmoor Military Railway was a vast organization responsible for training generations of soldiers in all aspects of railway construction and operation. Connecting Liss and Bordon (seen above in 1934), the network had its own stations and an entire railway infrastructure.

North British Railway Company.

Date_____191 5

ON WAR SERVICE

From SOUTH LEITH

To _LONGTOWN_

Via _____

Wagon_____ Sheet_____

Consigned_____

◄ World War I involved the railways on a massive scale. The Royal Engineers operated railways in many parts of the world. Training was usually undertaken at Longmoor. It is likely that this group, posing in front of an LSWR locomotive, have just finished their training.

▲ From 1916, when conscription was introduced, women increasingly took over jobs hitherto done by men, many on the railways. In 1917 a group of women at London's Liverpool Street Station display the uniforms of the various branches of the Great Eastern Railway.

► During the build-up to D-Day in 1944, railways were the prime movers of men and equipment, first to the concentration points and then southwards to the invasion ports. In April and May of that year over 24,000 special trains moved troops, ammunition and equipment, from tanks to bandages. Much of this was for the Americans, and during this time US Army Transport Corps locomotives ran on Britain's railways.

MILK TRAINS

The carriage of milk by train started in the 1830s but it remained a local activity until the emergence of large national wholesale and distribution companies, such as Express Dairies, founded in 1864. This was followed by the development of railhead milk depots, the first of which was opened in Wiltshire in 1871. Long-distance milk traffic became the norm towards the end of the 19th century, initially on passenger trains and then from the 1890s on special milk trains. All milk was transported in the familiar cans, or churns, owned by the dairy companies. Milk tank wagons were not introduced until 1927. Supplying the big cities with daily supplies of milk became the priority, reflecting concerns about improving the diet of the urban poor. By 1914 the railways were carrying 93 million gallons of milk into London each year; by the 1920s, over 260 million gallons. In 1942 the Milk Marketing Board took over and long-distance deliveries diminished. The last regular milk trains ran in 1980, then rail surrendered to road.

(5041 k)
GREAT WESTERN RAILWAY.
MILK
FROM

TO
BOW (L.M.S.)
VIA KENSINGTON

Date............... No. of Tank............... Train...............
6,000 BM. 884 4/47.

◀ The many scheduled special trains that transported milk in bulk were often assembled from tankers collected from a number of smaller depots. Here, at Leyburn, Wensleydale, in 1954 an LNER shunting locomotive attaches a few milk tankers to a waiting passenger train.

▶ Milk was not supplied for domestic use in glass bottles until well into the 20th century, when bottling plants were established at rail-based distribution depots. In the pre-bottle age, milk was sold in bulk, with customers fetching it in their own containers. This man is carefully making his way back to his house with his personal supply of milk.

The Calm Pleasures of the Pasturing Herd

◀ This idyllic rural scene, a popular subject for postcards through the first half of the 20th century, dates from 1907. At that time, the railways still played a major role in the cattle business. Cows were transported by train to and from market, and from farm to farm, and their milk was carried by train from the depots to the distribution centres, often over long distances. The carriage of meat was also a major part of the railway's activities.

▶ The role of the railway in the local farming community was always significant. Passenger trains regularly collected small numbers of milk churns from rural and branch line halts, such as Wanstrow, in Somerset, shown here. The traffic, of course, was two-way, with empty churns being transported by train back to the farmer.

Milk traffic at Highbridge, Somerset, in 1928. The lorry has collected the churns from the farms and they will now be loaded into the ventilated box vans. Cans, or churns, were of a standard conical shape, holding 17 gallons and weighing 2cwt when full. Later, smaller and more manageable cans were introduced.

MINIATURE RAILWAYS

The distinction between narrow-gauge and miniature railways is not clear, but the latter tend to be built to a gauge that is 18in or less. Miniature railways were first promoted in the late Victorian period by Sir Arthur Heywood, who built a 15in-gauge line on his estate near Derby to demonstrate the practical passenger- and freight-carrying possibilities of the miniature railway. His vision of a national network of miniature lines linking estates, villages and remote regions to the main lines was not to be realized, but by the Edwardian era the potential for tourism offered by such lines was being appreciated. However, the real heyday of the miniature railway was the 1920s and 1930s, with a notable example being the 15in-gauge Romney, Hythe & Dymchurch Railway in Kent. During this period many miniature railways were built, both as practical passenger-carrying lines and as tourist attractions. Indeed, there came a time when few seaside resorts and parks did not boast a miniature railway of some kind or another. Some used locomotives that were scaled-down versions of the real thing, while others adapted industrial vehicles. More common today, particularly among enthusiasts, are lines built to a smaller gauge, 7in or less, with passengers sitting astride the vehicles.

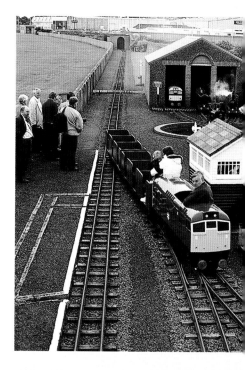

▲ Kerr's Miniature Railway opened as a tourist line in Arbroath, Angus, in 1935 and by 1937 it was carrying over 20,000 passengers per year. By the 1950s this had risen to 60,000, but a decline then followed and the line faced closure in the late 1970s. Since then it has been extensively restored and rebuil▶

◀ A typical enthusiasts' and model makers' miniature railway is the Heath Park line near Cardiff, photographed here in 1991. The locomotives used on such a line are normally meticulously-made scale models, such as the GWR 'Manor' shown here. Such lines, often run by clubs, are usually for demonstratio▶ purposes, and passengers make short journeys sitting astride the vehicles.

Built in 1895 as a 15in-gauge
line linking Fairbourne village
with Penrhyn Point, Gwynedd, the
Fairbourne & Barmouth Railway
has had a chequered career but is
now enjoying success once more.
Rebuilt to a smaller gauge in 1984,
the line is famous for its setting
and for its locomotives, which are
half-size replicas of classic narrow-
gauge engines.

◀ A typical seaside resort railway was built in
Southport, Lancashire, by George Llewellyn from
1911. With its scaled-down replica locomotives and
tall passenger vehicles, this was a proper miniature
railway, as indicated by this Edwardian postcard.

▶ A number of miniature railways
were built to serve private estates,
the first of these opened at the
Duke of Westminster's Eaton Hall,
in Cheshire, in 1898. These had both
practical and entertainment functions.
This Edwardian postcard shows
the Blakesley Hall line, a working
miniature railway built by CW
Bartholomew from 1903 to serve his
Towcester estate, in Northamptonshire.

MINIATURE RAILWAY, BLAKESLEY HALL

Named Trains

The first train in Britain to be given an official name was probably the Irish Mail, in 1848. Subsequently, many trains acquired unofficial names, a number of which started out as nicknames invented by members of staff. Typical of this was the Flying Dutchman, running between London and Exeter and named after a Derby-winning horse. In the late Victorian period Pullman and Club trains came into the schedules, but actual 'named trains' were still a rarity. An exception was the Cornish Riviera Express, introduced by the GWR in about 1905. The real expansion of the named-train network occurred in the 1920s, after the formation of the Big Four Grouping of railway companies, with the appearance of well-known, high-speed or luxury services such as the Royal Scot, the Atlantic Coast Express and the Golden Arrow. Many more were added during the 1930s, including the Coronation Scot and the Cheltenham Spa Express, whose nickname, the Cheltenham Flyer, soon achieved official status. After nationalization of the railways in 1948, naming was briefly abandoned, but was to return in force in the 1950s and early 1960s, when named trains were running to every part of Britain. Today, some names live on, but the dedicated named train has gone.

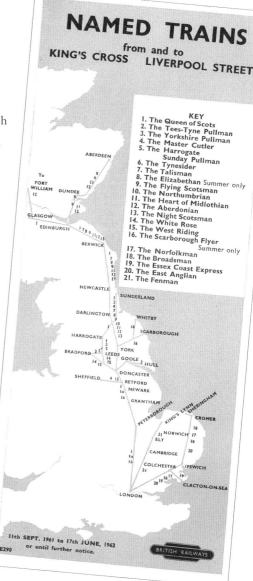

NAMED TRAINS
from and to
KING'S CROSS   LIVERPOOL STREET

KEY
1. The Queen of Scots
2. The Tees-Tyne Pullman
3. The Yorkshire Pullman
4. The Master Cutler
5. The Harrogate Sunday Pullman
6. The Tynesider
7. The Talisman
8. The Elizabethan Summer only
9. The Flying Scotsman
10. The Northumbrian
11. The Heart of Midlothian
12. The Aberdonian
13. The Night Scotsman
14. The White Rose
15. The West Riding
16. The Scarborough Flyer Summer only
17. The Norfolkman
18. The Broadsman
19. The Essex Coast Express
20. The East Anglian
21. The Fenman

11th SEPT. 1961 to 17th JUNE, 1962
E290   or until further notice.

BRITISH RAILWAYS

▲ This 1962 leaflet advertises 21 named trains running through the east of Britain from London's King's Cross and Liverpool Street. They range from the Queen of Scots to now forgotten expresses serving such places as Clacton and Whitby.

◄ One of the many named trains on the London to Scotland routes was the Waverley, seen here pausing at Leeds in 1960.

◄ In the 1950s, one of the most famous named trains, the Golden Arrow, waits to leave Victoria station for Dover, typically bedecked with arrows and flags. Operated in conjunction with a dedicated cross-channel ferry and the French Flèche d'Or, which ran between Calais and Paris, the all-Pullman service ran until 1972.

▼ Confusingly, the Flying Scotsman is both a famous locomotive and a famous named train. The latter was used in the 1870s but it was the LNER who first used it officially on a high-speed service to Scotland. In the 1960s, near the end of its life, the Scotsman was diesel-hauled.

WESTERN REGION
FAMOUS NAMED TRAINS

CORNISH RIVIERA EXPRESS
THE MAYFLOWER   THE BRISTOLIAN
TORBAY EXPRESS
THE SOUTH WALES PULLMAN   THE ROYAL DUCHY
CAPITALS UNITED EXPRESS   THE MERCHANT VENTURER
THE PEMBROKE COAST EXPRESS   CHELTENHAM SPA EXPRESS
THE CATHEDRALS EXPRESS   CAMBRIAN COAST EXPRESS
THE CORNISHMAN   THE INTER-CITY
THE RED DRAGON

13th JUNE to 11th SEPTEMBER 1960

▲ In 1960 BR's Western Region operated 15 named trains. These linked Paddington to Somerset, Devon and Cornwall, north and south Wales, Cheltenham, Hereford and Wolverhampton.

NAMEPLATES

The practice of naming locomotives goes back to the dawn of railways, perhaps echoing maritime traditions. However, with the rapid increase in the numbers of locomotives from the 1850s, more definite forms of identification became necessary and many railways were prompted to adopt numbers as well as names. Initially both were applied in a random manner, but as distinct classes of locomotives emerged, so systems were established for numbering and for naming. The first half of the 20th century was probably the golden age of naming. Inspiration for the names was drawn from a wonderfully diverse range of sources, some predictable, some less so. Inevitably some names were used often, some infrequently: 'Falcon' has been used thirteen times, 'Redwing' only once.

In the early years of British Railways the naming tradition was maintained, partly to make the changeover from steam to diesel more acceptable. More recently, naming has been a random process, usually only for short-term publicity. When locomotives die, their nameplates sometimes survive, a process that has generated a collectors' market.

◄ For those collectors who cannot afford the real thing, there are companies that make excellent full-size replica nameplates. An example is this 'Irresistible' plate, the original of which graced an LMS Jubilee locomotive built in 1936.

◄ Military and regimental names were well used. The LNER V2 class included many locomotives but only seven were named. This plate from no. 4806 'The Green Howard' was unveiled at Richmond, Yorkshire, in 1938.

▼ Nameplates are the top of the tree for railwayana collectors. This group, proudly displaying their plates, met at a private railway museum during 1986. Classic plates like these often command huge prices, often into to five figures.

'Beattie' was the name carried originally by a large tank locomotive built by the LB&SCR. In the 1930s these were rebuilt as the Remembrance class of tender locomotives. 'Beattie' ultimately became no. 32331.

The LNER introduced the D49 Hunt class locomotives from 1932. 'The Morpeth', no. 62768, was built at Darlington in 1934. The nameplates carried the distinctive running fox.

◄ 'Ben Cruachan' is a typical example of a later British Railways style of nameplate, carried originally by a class 37 diesel, 37404, built in 1965. Although less valuable than steam plates, diesels are still popular.

▼ Nameplates were made with great care, as this highly detailed works drawing indicates. Drawn in Doncaster in 1961, it relates to the plates for eight Deltic diesel locomotives that were to carry the names of famous racehorses: St Paddy, Ballymoss, Crepello, Meld, Nimbus, Pinza, Tulyar and Alycidon.

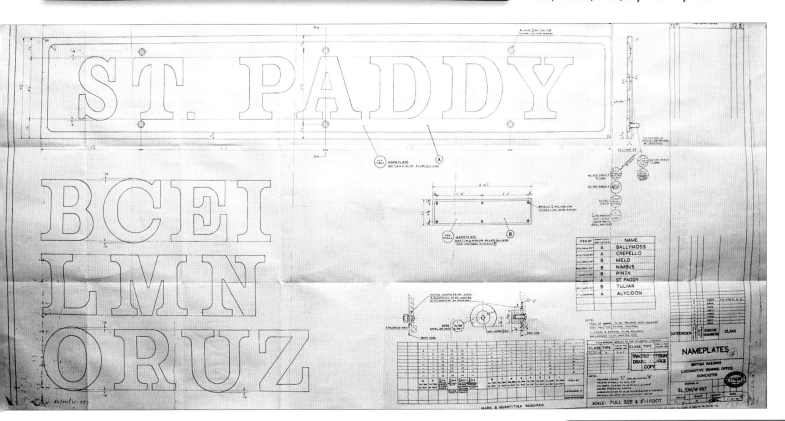

N ARROW-GAUGE LINES

The early railway builders used many gauges, to suit the needs of local industries. It was not until the 1860s that narrow gauge, that is to say 3ft or less, became established as a viable alternative to standard gauge. Reduced construction and operating costs, particularly in difficult terrain, added to the appeal of the narrow-gauge railway. Wales became the home of narrow gauge, even though the gauge itself was far from standard (2ft, 2ft 3in, 2ft 8in and 3ft were all in use). Lines were primarily industrial, for the transport of slate and other minerals, and passenger traffic was largely unimportant.

In England the national network was by then so comprehensive that there was little demand for narrow gauge except in local industries such as clay or stone. Later the rise of tourism and the passing, in 1896, of the Light Railways Act prompted a new enthusiasm for passenger-carrying narrow-gauge lines, with more than ten opening in various parts of Britain between the 1890s and the 1920s. At the same time, existing industrial lines turned themselves into tourist railways. In this new role, narrow-gauge railways flourished until the 1930s, when most went out of business.

▶ One of Britain's most remote narrow-gauge lines was the Campbeltown & Machrihanish in Scotland. Originally a coal line, it was rebuilt for passengers in 1906. It was never very successful, despite attractive publicity such as this card, and closed in 1932.

CAMPBELTOWN & MACHRIHANISH LIGHT · RAILWAY

TRAIN · LEAVES CAMPBELTOWN IMMEDIATELY · AFTER · PASSEN= =GERS · HAVE · LANDED · FROM STEAMER ·

TRAIN · LEAVES MACHRIHANISH · FOR CAMPBELTOWN 35 MINUTES · BEFORE SAILING · TIME · OF STEAMER

MACHRIHANISH ·

RETURN FARE 1/-

ENGINE · WHISTLE SOUNDS · 5 · MINUTES BEFORE · STARTING TIME · OF · TRAIN

TICKETS ISSUED ON STEAMER AND TRAIN

JOURNEY TAKES 20 MINUTES EACH WAY

STEAMER WAITS RETURN OF TRAIN FROM MACHRIHANISH

◀ Dinorwic was one of the largest of the Welsh slate quarries, served by an extensive narrow-gauge network and with mainline connections at Port Dinorwic. Slate wagons were hauled between quarry levels by inclined planes.

Port Dinorwic Incline, Slates arriving from Quarry

▲ Opened in 1859 to serve slate quarries in the hills above Machynlleth, the Corris developed in the 1880s an early interest in passenger-carrying. It also pioneered connecting bus services. Taken over by the GWR in 1930, it lost its passenger services in 1931 but freight traffic continued until 1948.

▼ In this classic image of an English narrow-gauge line, Lynton & Barnstaple locomotive 'Taw' hauls its train through the glorious Devon landscape. Opened in 1898, the railway closed in 1935.

Inset: Encouraged by Southwold Town Council, keen to bring visitors to its developing little resort, the Southwold Railway opened in 1879, with four trains a day linking with the main line at Halesworth. It prospered until the 1920s, when increasing competition from road transport brought it to an end in 1929.

SOUTHWOLD RAILWAY TRAIN.
SEP 1879 - APRIL 1929.

OLD CARRIAGES

When a railway carriage comes to the end of its life, the final resting place is usually the scrapyard. The chassis and running gear may be reused but the body is broken up or burned. It was ever thus. However, railway companies have always been aware that carriage bodies can be useful, so there is a long tradition of using them as stores, mess rooms, dormitories and even station waiting rooms.

It has also been known for decades that a railway carriage can be turned into an adequate home. This practice was at its peak in the 1920s, when a severe housing shortage after World War I coincided with the decision, taken for safety reasons largely as a result of the disaster at Quintinshill in 1915, to do away with wooden-bodied carriages. The process was helped by the lack of planning laws and by the railway companies' willingness to sell off redundant vehicles. Old carriages appeared in fields all over Britain, usually in ones or twos but sometimes in colonies, with famous examples at Shoreham and Selsey, in Sussex, and Dungeness, in Kent. Today only a small number of carriage homes survive, and time, weather and land values ensure that the number diminishes each year. A very few have been rescued after years of use as living accommodation and are back at work on preserved lines.

▲ There were many uses to which an old railway carriage could be put, apart from living accommodation. This one found a new life as a school annexe in Ackworth, to the east of Wakefield, in Yorkshire.

▼ This ex-LNER carriage, with several others, enjoyed for some years a new life on a siding at Newton Abbot, in Devon, as offices for the publishers of this book, David & Charles.

◄ A famous example of carriage reuse was to be seen for some years at Gatehouse of Fleet, in Dumfries & Galloway, where this long clerestory vehicle was in service as a church.

On many rural and branch lines, railway companies saved money by using carriage bodies as waiting rooms. This one was at Cutler's Green Halt, on the Thaxted branch, in Essex.

▲ Many farms all over the country still have the remains of railway goods vehicles quietly decaying in their fields and farmyards after a long and useful life as feed and tool stores or as livestock shelters. This cow looks quite at home with this former box-van in the corner of her Norfolk field.

Old railway carriages can be found all over Britain, with many still earning their keep as holiday homes. This example, smartly presented in LNER colours, is delightfully placed beside a stream in Yorkshire, having acquired a pitched roof to protect it from the worst of the weather.

OLD CARRIAGES

▶ Carriage cottages do still survive in surprising locations. This example, still recognizable despite extensive additions, is on a main road in South Wootton, near King's Lynn, in Norfolk. Maybe its active life was on the line to Hunstanton.

◀ Many old carriages extended their lives as camping coaches. In 1968 this former SE&CR royal saloon was one such at Glenfinnan, on the Fort William-to-Mallaig line.

▼ Another survivor lives on as a summer house in a private garden near Lessingham, not far from the Norfolk coast. Today, it is a long way from any railway but when it arrived decades ago it probably came from Stalham, a couple of miles away and then on the M&GN's Cromer-to-Yarmouth line.

▲ The family poses with the newly arrived carriages, delivered by horse-drawn carts.

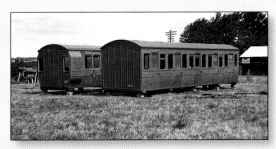

▲ The two bodies are placed side by side on the acre plot purchased for the new house.

Carriage cottages may survive, but their history is often lost. It is, therefore, a rare treat to be able to tell the full story of one that did not get away. The principle was that the railway company would sell the carriage body, and the price included its transport to a station of the buyer's choice. Transport from that station or goods yard to the site was the buyer's responsibility. In August 1923 this family took delivery of two old carriage bodies from the Southern Railway which, as the original invoice shows, was using up old LSWR stationery. The price for the two was £39. Remarkably, the house that was then built from these carriages is still owned by the same family, along with the photographs that document the arrival of the carriages and their conversion into a substantial holiday home.

▲ With the house finished, the carriages have almost disappeared. This survives unchanged.

▲ Construction starts on the roof that will span the two carriages.

▲ By 1924 the holiday home was in use, as this view of the living room shows.

PRIVATE WAGONS

Privately-owned wagons have always been a feature of railways in Britain, although in the very early days they were regarded with disfavour by some companies. The North Staffordshire, for example, refused to allow them on their networks. Problems arose because of differing manufacturing standards and specifications, and inadequate maintenance was held responsible for a number of accidents. Some of the larger companies, such as the Midland, tried to buy up privately-owned wagons but in 1914 there were still about 4,000 owners with wagons in use across the network. The majority were in the coal and mineral trades; others were built to carry chemicals, cement, gas, oil and petroleum products, milk, biscuits, mustard, bananas and even sausages.

Today privately-owned wagons are still widely used, for minerals, cement, oil and petrol, cars and many other products, but tend to be run as complete trains rather than individually. What has been lost is the wonderful diversity and the quirky individuality that added so much interest to goods trains and goods yards in the pre-British Railways era.

▶ The coal trade was the primary user of the private-owner wagon and hundreds of collieries and coal merchants had their names carried all over Britain on the sides of the standard planked, open wagon. This example is from Dennyloanhead, west of Falkirk.

◀ Tank wagons were the next most common type after the planked open wagon. Many were specially built for the oil, gas and petroleum trades. By this time, the rigid steel chassis and the running gear had been standarized.

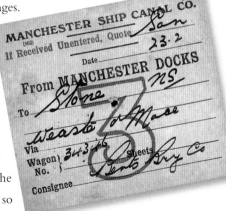

▲ The building of private-owner wagons was a highly competitive business, and companies often photographed or displayed newly completed vehicles for publicity purposes. This example belonged to the Birley coal company, whose collieries were near Sheffield.

Most private-owner wagons were fairly basic, but luxury vehicles designed for high-speed running did exist, particularly for the food industry. This 1930s six-wheeled wagon for Palethorpes sausages is typical, built to run on the LMS network.

Private-owner box vans were less common. Leith General Warehousing had a fleet of these distinctive apex-roofed, wooden vehicles for general cargo distribution.

This is a Welsh example of the typical wooden-bodied, open coal wagon, in this case owned by a coal merchant rather than a colliery.

The steel industry generally required steel-built wagons for durability and safety. At this point, such wagons had only hand brakes, for use from ground level, and train braking was down to the guard's van and the locomotive.

Proudly displayed by its builder, this high-sided, open wagon was the first to be completed for the Ipswich Gas Company. It would have been used for transporting coal and coke to and from the gas works. Despite this mundane local use, the vehicle shows the careful painting and finishing typical of the private-owner wagon.

PUBLICITY

In the Victorian period railway publicity tended to be direct and to the point, concentrating on routes, fares, timetables, excursions and so on, usually presented in bold typography. Ceramics and enamel were used for more durable notices. Colour-printed posters first appeared in the 1870s but it was not until the Edwardian era that these began to achieve a distinctive style and quality, coincidental with a more sophisticated view of advertising and publicity.

Before World War I, leading companies began to concern themselves about image and house style, and this trend became more apparent after the formation of the Big Four, all of which were highly design conscious. Posters were commissioned from leading artists, and great efforts were made to make stations tidier and more user friendly, and to ensure information was readily accessible. This approach was maintained by British Railways throughout the various changes of house style widely applied to publicity material from the 1950s until the 1980s. Illustrations and photographs were often combined with enterprising design to make memorable images.

▶ The British Rail image of the 1960s and 1970s maintained the traditions of the 1950s in the use of typography and illustrations but achieved a more modern look.

▼ Totally in the spirit of its age is this entertaining 1977 Motorail brochure, complete with butterfly and fantasy landscape, with a design approach reminiscent of the record covers of that time.

▲ In the 1950s clean typography, classic sans serif lettering and humorous illustrations were often combined to make even simple leaflets appealing.

▼ In the early 1960s British Railways produced a rather spicy set of travel posters promoting various holiday regions. The design was interesting and of its period, bringing together typography, illustration, collage – and, here, a sultry bathing beauty. At this point, the 1940s totem symbol was still in use, but it was on the way out.

Photographed in 1963, this enamel sign proved to be more durable than the railway promoted. The Maencloghog was an obscure and short-lived line, incorporated into the North Pembroke & Fishguard Railway. It was opened in 1898, operated by the GWR and, after a chequered career, closed in 1937. In World War II the line was used for target practice by the RAF and the USAF, and Maencloghog tunnel was used for training with Barnes Wallis' bouncing bombs.

◄ Some companies had route maps made in ceramic tiles for use at stations. A few survive, in effect living history. Historic too is the adjacent poster, a record of British Rail's long-gone holiday business.

PULLMANS

George Pullman developed the idea of the luxury railway carriage that bears his name in America and then brought it to Britain in the 1870s. Pullmans were owned, managed, maintained and staffed independently and were operated in conjunction with railway companies, who either added them to existing services or ran dedicated Pullman trains. Passengers paid a supplement, and service was superior to conventional first class, with food and drink served at-seat. Pullman's first British contract was with the Midland Railway in 1873 and other companies soon followed. Pullman died in 1897, by which time the Pullman carriage and train were well established, being operated by the Pullman Palace Car Company (from 1915 the Pullman Car Co.).

From the start, Pullmans were distinctive vehicles with flat body sides and vestibules at each end. There were several types, including parlour, restaurant and bar cars. The famous brown-and-cream livery with its ornate lining was established by 1906 and each carriage had a name or number emblazoned on the sides. From the 1920s British Pullman trains began to acquire names, usually based on the destination, such as the Brighton Belle or the West Riding Pullman, and this practice was maintained until the end of British Railways in the 1990s. Another popular use was as boat trains. In the meantime, in 1962, Pullman had become a part of British Railways. Until this date, Pullmans built in various railway workshops in Britain were all constructed and finished to the same standard, although there were minor variations in decoration. For example, some had marquetry panels, while others used lacquer, and styles ranged from 18th-century Revival to Art Deco.

▼ The most famous Pullman train, the Brighton Belle, ran from 1933 to 1972. Here, in its last year, it crosses Balcombe viaduct near Haywards Heath, Sussex, on its way to London Victoria.

► As an independent operator, the Pullman car company was responsible for its own publicity material, as this 1932 timetable indicates. In 1962 Pullman became part of British Railways but the name lives on, as this 1980 brochure for the Manchester Pullman shows. This also features the popular BRS logo of that period, 'This is the Age of the Train'.

PULLMAN CAR SERVICES

LONDON AND NORTH EASTERN RAILWAY

July 18th, 1932, and until further notice.

Every care and attention has been taken in compiling this leaflet in order that all the information given therein should be accurate. The Proprietors and Printers, however, disclaim any liability for loss or inconvenience occasioned by any possible inaccuracy.

Seats may be reserved and all information obtained at any of the Offices of Messrs. Thos. Cook & Son or The International Wagons-Lits Company, 20, St. James's St.

THE

Pullman Car Company, Ltd.

Victoria Stn., Southern Rly. (Eastern Sec.) London.

Telephone: VICTORIA 9278 (2 lines).

Printed by McCorquodale & Co. Ltd., London.

THE MANCHESTER PULLMAN

Pullma

This is the age of the train

From 1960 British Railways introduced an entirely new type of luxury train, the Blue Pullman, based on modern-looking, self-contained diesel electric train sets. Until 1973 these operated between London and Manchester, Bristol, Birmingham and Swansea. In the 1980s the final generation of Pullmans appeared, operated by British Rail's Intercity division. However, these were conventional first-class vehicles, with only the at-seat service being retained from the traditional Pullman concept, and were aimed largely at the business user. These came to an end with the destruction of British Rail in the privatization of the 1990s. Some classic Pullmans survive on special trains such as the Venice Simplon-Orient-Express.

In their heyday, classic Pullmans were often used for special trains carrying royalty or visiting heads of state, or for great state occasions such as the funeral of Sir Winston Churchill in 1965.

▼ In 1968 the Blue Pullman from London Paddington approaches Bristol, its destination. The road it crosses is choked with traffic: even then, it was quicker by train.

◀ Until the 1920s, the Pullman name was not always used to describe luxury express trains and there were many variations in the livery. This card shows the Hastings Car Train of about 1905, operated by the South Eastern & Chatham Railway.

▶ The Southern Belle, operated by the London, Brighton & South Coast Railway, was the precursor of the Brighton Belle. By 1910, the date of this card, the familiar brown-and-cream Pullman livery was established, to remain unchanged until the 1960s.

▼ The West Riding was a famous Pullman service, probably at its peak in the 1930s. Here, at some point in that decade, the down West Riding passes through Harringay, on the outskirts of London, hauled by A3 Pacific no. 2747.

The 1986 leaflet (inset) promotes the Tees-Tyne Pullman, one of the last generation of Pullman services operated by British Rail.

Tees-Tyne Pullman

The premier InterCity First Class service for the business traveller. Travel by Pullman at no extra cost, from Newcastle, Durham, Darlington or York to London.

13 January – 9 May 1986

We're getting there ⇄ InterCity

The QUEEN'S TRAIN

The first royal carriage was built by the London and Birmingham Railway in 1842, and other companies, notably the London & Birmingham and the South Eastern, which served routes used frequently by the Queen and the royal family, soon added royal vehicles to their fleets. These early, and rather uncomfortable, four-wheelers were soon replaced by large, more luxurious carriages, culminating in a 12-wheeler put into service by the LNWR in 1895. By this time royal trains (and there were always several of them) were composed of dedicated sets of specially-built vehicles catering for all the needs of the Queen, her family and staff. The arrangements for any royal journey were complex in the extreme, and frequently caused considerable disruption to timetabled services along the route. Queen Victoria travelled extensively around Britain during the celebration of her golden and diamond jubilees, in 1887 and 1897, and companies who carried her regularly, such as the Great Western, either built new royal trains or refurbished existing ones. These pictures show the train used by the GWR in 1897.

▼ The 1897 GWR royal train had a dedicated locomotive, suitably named 'The Queen'. Built in Swindon in 1894, no. 3041 was originally called 'Emlyn'.

Queen Victoria, [se]en here in 1887, [en]joyed train travel [b]ut insisted that [sp]eeds be kept [to] a maximum [of] 40mph. The [Ju]bilee celebrations [ca]used her [p]opularity to soar, [an]d she travelled [ex]tensively around [h]er kingdom.

◀ The interior of the royal saloon was sumptuous but discreet and finished to the highest standard. There were electric lights and a bell to summon the guard. This is the view into the Queen's compartment from the area used by the maids of honour.

▼ This view shows the rather more spartan interior of the guard's van, with kitchen and water-heating equipment, and the handbrake in the foreground.

◀ This is the Queen's saloon used in the [G]WR's royal train in 1897. It was usually [pl]aced fifth in the set of carriages, well [a]way from the noise and smoke of the [lo]comotive.

▶ Looking like the most luxurious first-class [ca]rriage, complete with framed prints on the [pa]rtition walls, this is actually the smoking [sa]loon, with gentleman's lavatory.

RIVER AND CHANNEL CROSSINGS

Between the 1840s and 1984 railways and shipping were closely connected. More than 50 railway companies owned or operated many hundreds of ships during that period, from Lake District and Clyde pleasure steamers and cross-Channel ferries to cargo vessels, dredgers and tugs. Railway companies also built or controlled ports and harbours all round the coast of Britain, and from these they operated scheduled passenger and freight services to Ireland, the Channel Islands, France and Belgium, Germany and the Netherlands, and Scandinavia.

The first railway-controlled shipping services were over the River Hull, across the Irish Sea from Holyhead, and over the Channel to France and the Channel Islands. The network grew rapidly as more railway companies started more and more services, often in direct competition with each other. As ever, the railways were

L.&N.W.S.S. SCOTIA LEAVING HOLYHEAD FOR DUBLIN (NORTH WALL)

B.D. No. 30150

ONE-DAY EXCURSION TICKET
Folkestone to Boulogne

1st CLASS. | Available by the Boats as advertised.

▲ SS Scotia was a LNWR ship on the Holyhead-to-Dublin service in the Edwardian era. This card was used to promote all LNWR services to Ireland via Holyhead on their 'magnificent steamers'. It gave journey times from Euston, for example to Galway at 14 hours.

L.&N.W. S.S. "SCOTIA" SMOKING CABIN. HOLYHEAD & DUBLIN SERVICE.

► This view of the SS Scotia's smoking cabin shows the standard of decor in railway ferries before World War I.

◄ There was always plenty of free promotional material. This 1960s lapel badge was issued by British and French Railways car ferries.

DRIVE-ON DRIVE-OFF
BRITISH AND FRENCH RAILWAYS CAR FERRIES

◀ Day trips across the Channel were always popular and for many of them passports were not necessary. This first-class Folkestone-to-Boulogne ticket was issued by the Southern Railway to Ronald Cross in June 1926. This was valid only on the 10.15am boat, so it would have been a short day in Boulogne.

The Glasgow & South Western was one of several Scottish railway companies with shipping interests. This Edwardian card promotes one of their latest vessels on the Clyde routes, the *Atalanta*, a fast, modern turbine ship.

◀ Services between Newhaven and Dieppe were operated jointly by British and French railway companies, and this continued until the demise of Sealink in 1984. The *Senlac* was in service in the late 1970s and early 1980s, maintaining the tradition of familiar ships dedicated to the route.

▼ An Edwardian view of the Ladies' Boudoir on the *SS Brighton*, the LB&SCR's latest turbine ship, used on the Newhaven-to-Dieppe run. This promotional card advertises a three-hour crossing. Today's takes four hours.

◀ There were several scheduled train ferry services, mostly from Dover or Harwich. This is a British Railways wagon label used on the Zeebrugge service.

LADIES' BOUDOIR, TURBINE S.S. "BRIGHTON," L.B. & S.C.R.

▼ This 1955 brochure promoting Channel Islands services has a period quality typical of British Railways.

▲ British Railways used stylish graphics to promote connecting services across Europe. This 1960 brochure covers travel to the French and Italian rivieras.

conscious of their image as well as their territory, so ships carried clear company branding. The competitive nature of the business was underlined by stylish posters and publicity material.

Particular types of ships also appeared. They were usually fast day boats, with comfortable passenger facilities, built for rapid journeys and a quick turnaround. Sleeping accommodation was available on longer routes. There were also train ferries and dedicated cargo vessels and, from the 1930s, car carriers, though the first drive-on, drive-off ships did not appear until the 1950s. Joint ventures were common between railway and independent shipping companies and internationally, with some cross-Channel services being operated by French or Belgian and British companies in tandem.

When British Railways came into being in 1948, it took control of all existing railway shipping services and gained the freedom to operate routes wherever and whenever it wanted. A degree of standardization was applied to new ships, but they were still up-to-the-minute and innovative vessels, and most of the pre-war routes continued to operate, along with some new ones. British Rail was an early user of the hovercraft, with its Seaspeed routes in 1966. In 1970 the Sealink brand was launched and applied to all shipping services, even the ancient Windermere pleasure steamers. Railway control of shipping services ended in 1984.

► By 1963, when this brochure was produced, most cross-Channel ships were car ferries. This promoted services from Dover, with the cost for a car starting at £3 (single).

▲► The Golden Arrow was always the style leader in cross-Channel travel. This elegant brochure (right) is from 1959, when the return fare was £16. 8s. Above is a luggage label designed to adorn the smartest suitcases.

IRELAND
via
HOLYHEAD
DUN LAOGHAIRE

STEAMER SERVICES

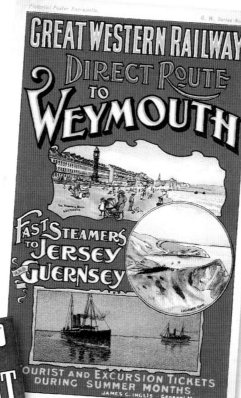

◄◄ This 1961 British Railways brochure gives details of the Holyhead-to-Dun Laoghaire services, with connecting trains to London. The ships boasted a Cabin de Luxe for £3 (first-class passengers only).

◄ Although Weymouth was served by both the GWR and the LSWR (and later the SR), the Great Western had control of the Channel Islands shipping services, as this Edwardian advertisement makes clear.

◄ From the early days, Hull was a major railway port, as this Edwardian NER promotional postcard indicates.

▼ Issued by British Rail's PR department in the 1970s, this photograph shows the newly modernized ferry terminal at Fishguard.

► This Edwardian advertising postcard promotes a new ship on the Channel Islands service and shows its lavish decor.

▼ British Rail's Seaspeed cross-Channel hovercraft services were introduced in 1966. In 1977 the sailings were still train-connected, and a single from London to Paris was £17.75.

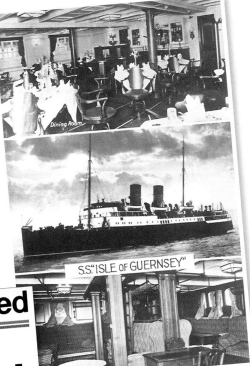

S.S. "ISLE OF GUERNSEY"

Seaspeed

Hovercraft services to
Paris and Brussels

May 2 - October 22 1977

► A 1947 Southern Railway brochure gives details of cross-Channel services for cars, motorcycles, caravans and baggage trailers. At this time, vehicles were still loaded by crane.

SOUTHERN RAILWAY
CONVEYANCE
OF
MOTOR CARS,
MOTOR-CYCLES,
CARAVAN & BAGGAGE TRAILERS
TO AND FROM
THE
CONTINENT
AND
CHANNEL ISLANDS

DOVER—CALAIS
FOLKESTONE—CALAIS
FOLKESTONE—BOULOGNE
DOVER—BOULOGNE
NEWHAVEN—DIEPPE
DOVER—OSTEND
SOUTHAMPTON—HAVRE
SOUTHAMPTON—CHANNEL ISLANDS
JERSEY—ST. MALO

SERVICES, RATES & FARES
BY ALL ROUTES

SUMMER—1947

Waterloo Station, S.E.1.

E. J. MISSENDEN, General Manager.

CALEDONIAN RAILWAY

◄ Ferry and pleasure steamer routes around the Clyde and the Scottish islands were very competitive, and a number of railway ran fleets of ships, including the Caledonian.

CALEDONIAN CLYDE TOURIST STEAMERS

◄ The Furness Railway was a small but ambitious railway whose wealth initially came from the exploitation of haematite deposits north of Barrow. Later, it was a pioneer in the development of tourism and became well known for its fleet of fast, modern pleasure steamers. This Edwardian card, published by the Furness itself, promotes their latest ship, the paddle steamer *Lady Moyra*.

▼ In 1959 the *Maid of Kent*, British Railways' latest and most modern cross-Channel ferry, came into service. Though small by modern standards, the *Maid* was at the time widely regarded as state of the art. These British Railways publicity photographs from May 1959 show the ship, the master's cabin, the restaurant and a cut-away drawing highlighting the two-storey car deck, the buffet and the restaurant.

THE FAST AND POWERFUL NEW STEAMER "LADY MOYRA," NOW ON THIS SERVICE.

Furness Railway.   P. S. "LADY MARGARET."   BARROW & FLEETWOOD.

S.S. MAID OF KENT CROSS CHANNEL CAR FERRY

ROYAL TRAINS

Queen Victoria first travelled by train on 13 June 1842, and she enjoyed the experience. She used royal trains extensively throughout her reign, particularly on journeys to Osborne, on the Isle of Wight, and Balmoral, in Scotland. Carriages were lavish and comfortable, specially built by various railway companies. From the late 1840s they were fitted with a lavatory. The organization of royal train journeys was complex, involving different companies and compounded by security concerns and the Queen's insistence on a 40mph maximum speed. Subsequent monarchs continued to use royal trains regularly, making the most of new vehicles as they were introduced and travelling at normal speeds. The royal family always paid to use the trains, and invoices indicate that even the dogs were charged for.

Today the royal train, completely refurbished in 1985, is used from time to time, although it is regularly threatened with the axe. It survives simply because it still offers a high degree of comfort, security and privacy.

▶ This timetable, issued to passengers on a royal train in May 1955, shows the meticulous planning involved in a royal journey, including the overnight stop.

BRITISH RAILWAYS

TIME TABLE

MONDAY, 2nd MAY, 1955

Wolferton	dep.	10.5 p.m.
King's Lynn	{ arr.	10.15 "
	{ dep.	10.22 "
Peterborough (East)	{ arr.	11.35 "
	{ dep.	11.50 "

TUESDAY, 3rd MAY, 1955

Rugby	pass	1.26 a.m.
Birmingham (New Street)	{ arr.	2.10 "
	{ dep.	2.25 "
Broom Junction (Night Halt)	{ arr.	3.30 "
	{ dep.	8.45 "
Cheltenham Spa (Lansdown)	pass	9.43 "
Gloucester (Central)	arr.	10.0 "
Gloucester (Central)	dep.	3.35 p.m.
Kemble	{ arr.	4.15 "
	{ dep.	4.21 "
Swindon Junction	pass	4.45 "
Didcot	"	5.13 "
Reading (General)	"	5.32 "
London (Paddington)	arr.	6.15 "

▶ The LNWR built a new royal train for Edward VII and Queen Alexandra, with a notably contemporary look to its interior decoration and fittings, and every modern convenience. Justifiably proud, the company displayed it in a series of official postcards. These cards show the light, spacious and informal style of Queen Alexandra's sleeping compartment.

HIS MAJESTY'S SLEEPING COMPARTMENT.

LONDON & NORTH WESTERN RAILWAY

HER MAJESTY'S SLEEPING COMPARTMENT

▲ A lucky enthusiast is on the spot to film the royal train passing Wormald Green, near Harrogate, in May 1967. The carriages and the Jubilee-class locomotive 'Alberta' suggest an earlier period.

◄ On a summer's day in 1986 the recently refurbished royal train passed through Llandrindod Wells on the Central Wales line, hauled by an immaculate class 47 diesel.

SCULPTURE

Many of those associated with the building and running of railways are commemorated by statues and memorials. Stephenson and Brunel have several, but many lesser figures are also remembered, along with those killed in accidents. Most of these statues and memorials date from the 19th century, a period when sculpture was considered important. Sculpture was commonly associated with architecture, and a number of major city station buildings have significant sculptural decoration.

The most striking railway sculptures are war memorials. Thousands of railway employees were killed in both World Wars and their sacrifice is commemorated on stations all over the country. These memorials are usually in the form of plaques listing the names, but at some stations they took the form of major works in bronze or stone by leading artists. There are impressive examples in London, at Euston, at Waterloo, in the form of a Victory Arch, and at Paddington, where CS Jagger's great soldier figure commands platform 1.

◄ Sculptures honouring particular individuals are comparatively rare on stations. This is a relief portrait of JH Renton on Rannoch Moor in Scotland. Renton was a great supporter of this wild and remote line.

▼ Dover Marine station is now a car park but the building survives, along with the magnificent war memorial by W King, a winged Victory commemorating the employees of the SER killed in World War I.

A few things escaped the wholesale destruction of London's Euston station, notably Baron Carlo Marochetti's large 1870 bronze of Robert Stephenson, now sited outside the new building.

There was always rivalry between the two adjacent stations at Victoria in London, run by different companies, and this was maintained in the rebuilding that took place in the Edwardian era. In 1908 Reginald Blomfield designed a new façade for the South Eastern & Chatham Railway's eastern part of the station. This was a splendidly extravagant, French-style structure in white, highly-sculpted Portland stone, complete with paired pediments carried by powerful and bare-chested caryatid figures.

LONDON & NORTH-WESTERN RAILWAY MEMORIAL.
IN GRATEFUL MEMORY OF 3719 MEN OF THE L. & N-W. RLY. CO.
WHO FOR THEIR COUNTRY, JUSTICE AND FREEDOM SERVED AND DIED
IN THE GREAT WAR, 1914-1919.
THIS MONUMENT WAS RAISED BY THEIR COMRADES AND THE COMPANY
AS A LASTING MEMORIAL TO THEIR DEVOTION.

▲ This postcard commemorates the unveiling by Earl Haig on 21 October 1921 of the memorial to the 3,719 men of the LNWR killed in World War I. Designed by R Owen, it is a powerful sculpture in the form of an obelisk guarded by four bronze servicemen. It still stands in its original position outside Euston station.

SIGNALS

One of the most familiar features of the railway landscape was the semaphore signal. Standing alone or in small groups, or arranged en masse on a massive gantry across the track, signals were the visible sign of order and control. Signalling started with men waving flags or lamps but a more permanent system soon became necessary.

Throughout the Victorian period, signalling gradually improved with the drive towards greater clarity, efficiency and standardization usually inspired by accidents. By the end of the 19th century the two types of semaphore signal, red-and-white for home and yellow-and-black with a fishtail end for distant, were widely established, along with their accompanying lights.

From the 1860s, signals were increasingly controlled from signal boxes, interlocked with points. The authority and control of the signalman was established formally in 1889 when block working and interlocking were made compulsory. Colour light signalling was first used in the 1920s, then spread rapidly over the network. However, the semaphore signal was still in widespread use in the 1980s, and even today many survive on secondary and goods lines.

◄ A classic and once universal railway scene: the signalman stands at his door and surveys his domain, which include the paired home and distant signals in the foreground.

▲ Despite consta improvements and moves towards standardization, many old or unusual semaphor signals survived, in many cases reflecting the individuality of the pre-Grouping era. This one was photographed at Cheam, Surrey, in 1937.

◀ On some single lines, such as the Hayling branch, signals faced both ways. Despite all the smoke, the train was unlikely to exceed the 20mph limit.

▼ The most impressive signal gantries were not necessarily at the largest stations. This magnificent example was at Alnwick, Northumberland, seen here controlling the arrival of the passenger train from Alnmouth, hauled by class J39 no. 64897.

◄ An ancient signal surviving on an ancient railway, photographed in 1962 near Whimsey Halt on the Forest of Dean line to Bullo Pill. The embankment behind used to carry the Severn & Wye line to Cinderford, closed in 1958.

► While signals were meant, for safety reasons, to be all the same, there were, in fact, infinite variations, determined often by the setting. Another mark of individuality was the iron or wood finial, which often had defined company characteristics.

▲ In 1968 steam and diesel meet either side of Preston's massive signal gantry.

► In 1967 a football special, under the control of a Britannia class 4-6-2, no. 70010, 'Owen Glendower', races towards Mallerstang signal box while the signal, on a post heightened for visibility, indicates an approaching train.

Signalmen

After the train driver, the most familiar figure in popular railway lore is the signalman, solitary in his box over long hours of day and night and in all weathers, controlling the safe passage of trains. Initially policemen controlled signals, while dedicated pointsmen looked after the points. With the introduction of interlocking and block systems, it all came together under one man, working in a specially built cabin or box and responsible for one length of track. The application of complex rules and

◄ Signalmen tended to be a particular breed of man, self-contained, at ease with his own company and able to enjoy the particular qualities of the job. Often they were friendly towards visitors, like this jolly chap at Scout Green, near Shap, photographed in the 1970s.

▲ Mr Richards, signalman at Binegar on the Somerset & Dorset railway, posed in his box for Ivo Peters, one of Britain's best-known railway photographers, in 1953.

regulations, and meticulous recording of all train movements and all messages sent or received, were the signalman's responsibility. He made decisions on prioritizing trains, particularly at junctions and on busy lines with a mix of freight and passenger services.

▲ Until the 1970s, signal boxes, and signalmen's duties, had changed little since the Victorian era. In most boxes, points and signals were still controlled by heavy levers, and messages were sent and received via telegraph block instruments. This classic view shows the signalman hard at work in his box at Desford Junction, in Leicestershire, on May 1963.

Signal Boxes

Though not yet extinct, the signal box is, thanks to modern electronics, an endangered species. Only a few hundred survive from the many thousands that used to exist. It is hard to imagine that something so close to the heart of railway history, and so familiar, will eventually disappear from the national network. In due course the signal box will follow the steam locomotive into that Jurassic Park of the railway, the preserved line. The signal box emerged in the 1860s, with the development of interlocking machinery that connected the control of signals and points, and then spread steadily over the network. The typical box was a two-storey structure, with the machinery on the ground floor, housed in brick or

▼ When photographed in 1984, Bardon Hill box, near Coalville, in Leicestershire, was a classic, in a remarkable state of repair, and still with its original nameboard. In the old days, signal boxes were often well kept, mainly because they were manned all the time.

▲ Firsby North, a box on the line between Boston and Louth, was looking a bit past its best in 1970. A typical timber-upper and brick-lower box, with decorative woodwork, it still boasted its nameboard and fire-bucket.

stone, and the levers and working space in the upper storey, which was usually made from wood. In principle, as they performed identical functions, all signal boxes could be the same. In practice, there was an infinite variety, and therein lay the box's enduring appeal. There was a huge range of sizes, shapes and settings, and great diversity of styles, many of which made the most of decorative timberwork. Bargeboarding, fretwork, finials and unusual window detailing, all played a part as railway companies relished the challenge of making individual something mundane and apparently predictable. There are echoes of fashionable architectural styles, from Gothic to Art Deco. Signalmen needed good all-round vision, a practical working space and creature comforts such as a stove, a cooker and, in later years, a lavatory.

▼ At Barton Street Junction by Gloucester's Eastgate station the box was set high on the gantry like a crow's nest, to ensure good visibility for the signalmen. Such arrangements were not unusual. Despite the functional nature of its position, the box still has decorative window frames and a roof finial.

◄ Roxton Box was built to control a level crossing and agricultural sidings near Stallingborough, on the Grimsby-to-Doncaster Line. The box, which survives, features an unusual style of timber construction.

London Midland and Scottish Railway Company.

CODE OF RINGS FOR FOG BELL

BETWEEN

SIGNAL BOX & STATION MASTER'S HOUSE

AT

PLUMPTON.

	RINGS.
Attention Signal ...	1
Lampman required ...	2
Fogsignalmen required ...	3
Assistance or Station Master required ...	4
Testing Bell Signal ...	16

The Attention Signal must be sent before any of the above codes are given, and such signal must be repeated at short intervals until replied to. Each code must be acknowledged by repetition to show that it is correctly understood, and if incorrectly repeated, must be given again until a correct reply is received.

Should any accident or obstruction occur, rendering assistance necessary, or should the Station Master be required, the Signalman will give 4 rings, and the Station Master must at once proceed to the Signal Box.

The Station Master must give the Testing Signal.

Any failure of the electric bell must be at once reported to the Electrical Department.

BY ORDER
of the
CHIEF GENERAL SUPERINTENDENT.

September, 1929.

► While much of the Isle of Wight's railway system was quiet and rural, Newport, at the network's heart, was a busy place. This box, with its pretty bargeboarding, controlled an important group of signals and points.

▼ In its heyday, Newton Abbot, Devon, was a major interchange station, handling busy passenger and goods traffic for both main and branch lines. The signal box was, therefore, a substantial building, and surprisingly large for one built from wood. The state of the box in 1984 reflects the station's relative decline since the 1960s.

Boxes came in all shapes and sizes and the smaller ones often controlled just a level crossing or a few sets of points. The delightfully named Chapel of Ease Crossing was by the Duffryn Yard in Port Talbot. In September 1963, this dedicated enthusiast has obviously carried out an inspection.

▲ When lines closed, signal boxes were generally stripped of their machinery and fittings but the buildings often remained, to be gradually destroyed by weather and vandals. This is the former box at St Briavels & Llandogo, on the Chepstow-to-Monmouth line, originally a handsome stone-built structure. As can be seen, the crossing gates had also survived in February 1966, when this photograph was taken.

◀ By 1973 the little Thorp Hall box was well past its best and was even looking rather derelict. Yet there are plenty of signs of activity and two railwaymen can be seen inside – as well as tea-making equipment, an essential part of signal-box life.

SPORTS SPECIALS

Most mass spectator sports were developed by the Victorians, with the railways playing a major role. The popularity of football soared after the establishment of the League and the Championship, both of which encouraged the large-scale movement of spectators by train – the famous Cup Final of 1923 at Wembley Stadium attracted over 200,000 fans, most of whom travelled by train. Football grounds, which were often in city centres, were usually located near railways; some had their own station, for example West Bromwich Albion's Hawthorn Halt. Football specials, started by railway companies in the 1880s, were immensely successful until the 1990s, when escalating vandalism and drunkenness brought them to an end.

Horse racing is a much older sport than football

► The great days of Charlton and Blackpool are recalled by this football excursion leaflet issued by the LMS in 1938. This so-called day trip would have tested the dedication of the fans, for they had to leave Euston at 1.30am and did not get back to London until 5am the next morning.

▼ In March 1967, near the end of the steam age, a football special approaches Leeds. Fans lean out and lavatory paper streams from the windows. By the late 1980s trains were regularly vandalized, and football specials soon ceased to run.

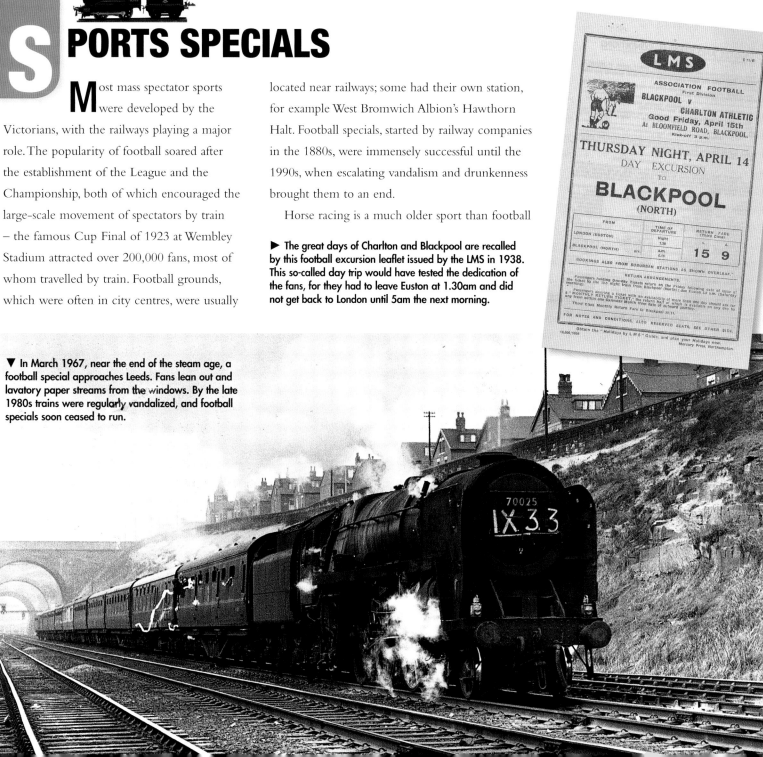

LMS

ASSOCIATION FOOTBALL
First Division
BLACKPOOL v
CHARLTON ATHLETIC
Good Friday, April 15th
At BLOOMFIELD ROAD, BLACKPOOL.
Kick-off 3 p.m.

THURSDAY NIGHT, APRIL 14
DAY EXCURSION
TO
BLACKPOOL
(NORTH)

◄ A crowded diesel multiple unit sets off for a day at Redcar races in the early 1960s, maintaining a tradition of racing specials set in the mid-Victorian era. The railways democratized racing by making it accessible to the masses and, by doing so, can be said to have prompted the development of the enclosure, in which to contain them.

But it was to the railways that it owed its rapid expansion in the 19th century. Racecourses near railways flourished, and some, including Newbury, Cheltenham and Newmarket, had dedicated stations. Horses were transported by rail in horseboxes until the 1970s. Race day excursions were a significant source of income, and even today Waterloo is awash with smart hats in Ascot week and on Derby Day.

(4) (58)
Stock
748 FF

SOUTHERN RAILWAY.
EMPTY HORSE BOX
CLEANSED & DISINFECTED

At_____
Date_____
To_____

Date_____
Vehicle No._____

► This 1964 leaflet underlines the popularity of Derby Day. It points out that Tattenham Corner station is right on the racecourse, which even today is heavily railway dependent.

British Railways
SOUTHERN REGION

EPSOM
RACES

Tuesday, Wednesday & Thursday
April 21st, 22nd & 23rd

Tuesday, Wednesday, Thursday & Friday
June 2nd, 3rd, 4th & 5th
(DERBY DAY WEDNESDAY, JUNE 3rd)

Saturday & Bank Holiday Monday
August 1st & 3rd

Friday & Saturday
September 4th & 5th

Frequent Train Services
TO
TATTENHAM CORNER
(ON THE COURSE)
EPSOM DOWNS
OR
EPSOM

FOR DETAILS OF FARES FROM LONDON AND A SELECTION
OF SUBURBAN STATIONS — SEE OTHER SIDE

- 8 MAY 1964

STONE, SLATE AND OTHER MINERAL TRAFFIC

The railways have always been important carriers of bulk cargoes, and in the early years most lines were built for the transport of minerals, notably stone and wall. These cargoes dominated goods traffic during the 19th and 20th centuries, and even today still represent the major part of a modern railway's freight business.

Stone

In the 18th century quarries were pioneer users of primitive, horse-drawn railways, so it is no surprise that they were among the first to use trains in the early decades of the railway age. Local quarry lines soon opened in many parts of Britain, and by the 1850s many railway companies were realizing the potential that lay in moving stone in bulk over long distances. As a result local stones such as Bath, Portland and Scottish granite began to be used in building projects far afield. Later, with a rapid increase in demand for crushed stone for road building, railways again made the most of the opportunity by developing limestone quarries in Derbyshire, Durham, Yorkshire, Somerset and elsewhere.

▲ Quarries frequently have their own railway system, for loading and marshalling the hoppers. In the past this was a well-known habitat of the industrial steam locomotive. Some survived in use long after the end of steam on the main lines, but today it is all diesel, as seen here at British Gypsum's Mountfield quarry.

◄ As this photograph makes clear the Derbyshire dales have been scarred by centuries of quarrying on a massive scale, and never more so than in the years since the coming of the railways. In the dramatic landscape of Miller's Dale on a summer's day in 1989, a line of hoppers filled with crushed limestone is hauled slowly from the quarry by a pair of class 37 diesels in contrasting liveries.

A number of lines, for example Buxton to Ashbourne, were built primarily for stone traffic, and many quarries were railway-owned. Today, a number of quarries, not least Merehead in Somerset, still give the railways plenty of business.

Railways themselves have always been major users of stone, both for the initial building of the network and continuously, for trackbed ballast, which is usually crushed limestone or granite, often from dedicated quarries such as Doveholes in Derbyshire or Meldon on Dartmoor.

Slate

Although some had been in operation for centuries, the slate quarries of Britain were a Victorian phenomenon. Huge quantities of slate were produced: over 500,000 tons from Wales alone in 1898, the year of peak production. Not only did slate cover the buildings of Britain, it also was exported to many parts of the world. The quarries were generally inland, so railways were needed to transport the finished slates to the quayside. They came early, in railway terms, particularly in north Wales. The Penrhyn network started

in 1801, Dinorwic in 1824 and Ffestiniog in 1836. These were narrow-gauge systems using gravity, rope haulage and horses to move the slate wagons. Steam came later, but the quarry railways remained self-contained, with idiosyncratic locomotives, rolling stock and operating practices, and with no link to the national network until the 1850s. Standard-gauge railways did not reach Blaenau Ffestiniog until 1879. Mainline railway connections encouraged the rapid expansion of the quarries, in Wales, Cornwall, the Lake District and Scotland, and by 1900 more slate was being transported by train than by ship. The industry declined steadily through the 20th century, with most of the major slate

▲ Slate quarry railways were quite distinct, with their own type of locomotive and a variety of specially designed wagons. Many of these remained in use for decades. Here, a line of loaded wagons travels along the main line in the Penrhyn system in 1961.

Locomotives meet on the Dinorwic network in 1956, while a visiting enthusiast adjusts his camera. Dinorwic was a huge quarry and the first to use railways. The locomotive in the foreground has survived into preservation.

Clay

Clay deposits in Purbeck, in Dorset, and north Devon have been exploited for centuries but it was not until the early 1800s that railways were used to transport the clay from the pits to the harbours. Extensive

networks of narrow- and standard-gauge lines were developed in the Victorian era, and these continued to flourish at least until the 1960s, serving harbours such as Poole, in Dorset, and Fremington, in north Devon, from where the clay was shipped to other British and European ports. This traffic had finished by the early 1980s. In many parts of Britain, but on a much more localized basis, brickmakers also used the railways to transport clay in bulk from the pits to the brickworks.

▲ Most brickworks were adjacent to huge clay pits, many of which were railway-operated. Typical was Southam, near Rugby, where the 1903 locomotive 'Jurassic' was still at work in 1954 hauling clay hoppers. Now preserved, 'Jurassic' lives at the Bala Lake Railway.

▼ Despite the loss of passenger services decades ago, Fowey is still a busy rail centre, servicing the clay trade. China clay from the massive deposits in Cornwall, used in papermaking, pharmaceuticals and many other industries as well as ceramics, is a major export cargo. Here, in the 1980s, a train of Fowey-bound clay wagons passes through Golant.

NORTON HILL COLLIERY. MIDSOMER NORTON 10450

► The main areas of coal production were the Midlands, north-east England, south Wales and Scotland, but there were also significant deposits in Somerset and Kent. The scale of demand and improvements in deep mining technology meant that relatively small deposits could be exploited. A typical small pit was Norton Hill, in the Somerset coalfield.

The South Kirkby, Featherstone, & Hemsworth Collieries, Ld.

FROM

HEMSWORTH COLLIERIES

L.N.E. and L.M.S. Rlys.

To .... (L.M.S. Stn.,

Via CR.....TON & NORMANTON,

For M ....

Wagon No. .... Weight ...... | TONS. | CWTS.

Date 192

▲ On every journey, every wagon had to carry a label showing its ownership, its route and destination, and the weight of coal carried. By this means haulage fees could be calculated and recorded, along with the location of the wagon. In the pre-computer age, this process required a massive bureaucracy, with all the information being collected and recorded by hand.

More significant, and very much alive today, is Cornwall's china clay industry, which has flourished since the late 18th century, when the deposits were first discovered.

Coal

Through the 1800s and up to the 1950s, Britain was a coal-fired country. The burning of coal, in various forms, powered industry, drove ships and railways, and heated homes, offices, shops, schools, churches and hospitals. The transport of coal from the mines to the docks and other distribution centres was, therefore, the major incentive for the building of railways, on both a local and a national scale. The financial success of many railway companies depended on the coal trade. From the 1850s the annual tonnage carried by rail rose steadily, reaching a peak of 225 million tons in 1913, with much of that being exported to markets all over the world. While the bulk of this traffic was transported to docks and depots, coal was also an essential domestic commodity. Every town, village, hamlet and farm needed coal, and this was delivered to local yards and stations by the wagon load. The wagons, owned by the railways, the collieries or the coal merchants, had to be emptied quickly and returned, so the movement of coal trains was continuous.

TICKETS

In its infancy, railway ticketing was a complicated and time-consuming process involving handwritten slips torn from receipt books – hence the origin of the term booking office. However, this system was open to abuse and inadequate for record-keeping. These problems came to the attention of Thomas Edmundson, a stationmaster working for the Newcastle & Carlisle Railway. He developed a system of standardized, serially-numbered, cardboard tickets with pre-printed destinations; the tickets could be mechanically dated when issued. They had three functions: to act as a receipt for the passenger's fare, to authorize a specific journey on a specific date, and to ensure that the railway company received all the money it was due (serial numbering meant that clerks had to account for every ticket). Edmundson moved to the Manchester & Leeds Railway in 1839 and that company quickly adopted his system over all its routes. Two years later he left, to set up with his son his own ticket business.

From the 1840s, the Edmundson system was

▲ The size of the Edmundson ticket was standard, but each company had its own style. These Edwardian tickets show the key features, the printed numbers and dates.

◀ The barrier, seen here at Loughborough Midland in the 1920s, has always been a vital element in the process of ticket checking and control. Today, it is done with electronic gates and tickets with magnetic strips.

adopted by railway companies all over Britain with Edmundson receiving a royalty. In principle, this system remained in use throughout the British railway network until 1990, when the standard green, pre-printed cardboard ticket finally disappeared. While green dominated the 20th century, it was by no means the only colour. In the pre-Grouping era all colours were used, with variations from company to company and to

► Stocks of old tickets often lasted for years. Here, in 1952, British Railways were still using up stocks of pre-nationalization GWR weekly season tickets.

▼ In the early days, tickets were sold at pubs and hotels. In some small stations, such as Farrington Gurney, near Radstock, this habit lingered on when the office – as often happened – was closed. Perhaps the dog needs a ticket.

▲ A ticket office at a large station was a busy place, with clerks working shifts. This BR photograph shows Southend Victoria in August 1961, with the walls still filled with racks of Edmundson tickets for every available destination and type of use.

◄ ▲ From the 1980s various types of machine-printed ticket were used by British Rail, though the names of smaller stations had to be filled in by hand. From the early 1990s the APTIS system took over.

denote different classes and different types of ticket – single or return, child, workman, military, excursion, platform, dog, cycle and so on. The recording of each ticket and its number was a heavy burden on the booking clerk. Despite this, and despite early attempts at improving the ticket-selling process, including coin-operated ticket machines, British Railways did not develop a system that printed tickets at the point of sale until the 1950s. This was brought into wider use in the 1960s, but still Edmundson survived in many parts of the network. It was the computer that finally changed the 150-year-old system when, after trials with various technologies, British Rail introduced APTIS (All Purpose Ticket Issuing System), whereby all ticket-selling machines are linked to a central computer. A portable version, SPORTIS, is used by guards issuing tickets on trains.

Technology apart, the booking or ticket office is still the most unchanged part of the station. Passengers still wait in queues to be served by a clerk behind a window, exactly as they did in the 1840s. There have been many variations in style and structure, and sometimes there were separate offices or windows for different classes or railway companies. At some big stations there could be up to six booking offices, and passengers needed to know both their place and their railway geography. Today, ticket offices are travel centres, and railways encourage online and advance booking – but it will take many years before the old Victorian habit of turning up, buying a ticket and getting on the train is finally broken.

▲ Platform tickets are largely a thing of the past, thanks to computers and the electronic barrier. However, modern examples can still be found.

▲ Preserved railways, as part of their period re-creation, continue to use Edmundson tickets, both for journeys and for the platform, though these are often souvenirs.

◀ The clerks in the booking office had many responsibilities beyond selling tickets including taking seat reservations and applying them to the right train.

▶ Large stations had separate luggage offices but in smaller ones the booking office clerks also had to organize passengers' luggage, much of which travelled in advance.

◀ This carefully posed photograph, notable for its unusually high staff/passenger ratio, shows ticket-checking at the barrier at Leicester London Road station in the 1930s.

TICKET OFFICE →

▲ Giving information was one of the many duties of the booking office clerks, so they had to know about all the special offers and excursions that were constantly dreamed up by the marketing people and then promoted with leaflet displays in the ticket office. This example, with the entertaining graphics of its era, offers cheap day tickets in October 1961.

In Victorian times the platform was a controlled area and people needed tickets even if they were not travelling. The platform ticket, varied in style and often bought from the once-familiar red penny-in-the-slot machine, remained a necessity for platform visitors through the 20th century.

TRACK REPAIRS

From the early days of the railways, maintenance of the track and the railway infrastructure was undertaken manually by gangs of platelayers or 'gangers', sometimes also known as waymen or – as in modern parlance – permanent way men or trackmen. A gang, under the control of a foreman and with a lookout armed with a hooter and flags, would be responsible for a length of track, usually a couple of miles, to be inspected twice a day, and maintained as required. Using a range of hand tools, they were responsible for the alignment, gauge and level of the track, for replacing sleepers, rails or chairs as necessary, for adjusting ballast, for checking points and for maintaining drains, culverts and lineside fences. Tools and equipment were kept in platelayers' huts placed regularly along the track, and often equipped with a stove. The derelict remains of these can still be seen all over the network. Trolleys were used for the transport of tools and materials. Major engineering works involved larger gangs and the closure of the line, usually at weekends. In 1948 over 60,000 permanent way men were employed by British Railways.

From the 1960s, mechanization, prefabricated welded track and new technology completely changed the world of track maintenance. By the 1990s there were 12,000 track maintenance staff, and now the work is done by outside contractors.

◀ In 1956 two gangers pause from their track-maintenance work on a stretch of the Welshpool & Llanfair narrow-gauge railway, then a public railway but now a famous preserved line.

▼ A permanent way gang poses for the camera in 1950, taking a break from laying a new stretch of track. At this date, this was an arduous and largely manual task.

Weed control was part of the platelayers' regular workload until weed-killing trains were introduced in the 1930s. Here, Southern Railways uses retired locomotive tenders to distribute the liquid.

◀ The weed-killing train is part of the regular pattern of track maintenance. In August 1993 a weed-killing train passes the old Maentwrog Road station on the Trawsfynydd branch in north Wales, now itself closed.

TRAINSPOTTERS

From the earliest days of railways, trains were regarded as objects of curiosity and fascination, with the locomotive the focus of popular interest. Largely for practical operating reasons, locomotives have usually carried names or numbers. Initially these were applied in a random manner, by the many independent railway companies. With the formation of the 'Big Four' railway companies in 1923, however,

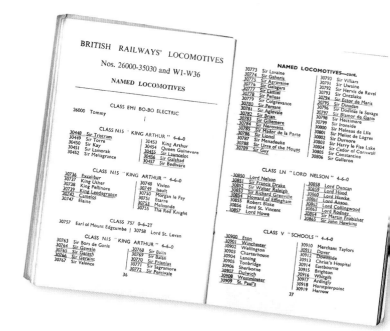

numbering was rationalized, and so the trainspotter was born. Since then the sight of small, and not so small, boys standing on platforms and recording train numbers and names has been a feature of the railways in Britain. While a major station or terminus was the preferred spotting location for many, others enjoyed the more limited, but more leisurely, qualities of the rural railway or branch line, where unusual, elderly or rare locomotives and vehicles might be seen.

With the advent of British Railways came the introduction of a national numbering system. This encouraged a great expansion of trainspotters' handbooks, most famously the Ian Allan *ABC* series, show above. For a trainspotter, nothing could eclipse the excitement and sense of triumph that followed the recording of the last missing locomotive from a particular class or group.

◀ For many children a railway is irresistible and hours can happily be spent watching trains. Indeed, for many children this is the start of something that turns into a lifelong enthusiasm, or even passion. Such an apprenticeship is common among railway historians. This small boy, photographed in the 1970s as he watches the passage of an ordinary diesel railcar on the Severn Beach branch at Ashley Hill, near Bristol, may now be such a person.

◄ Some young enthusiasts grow up to become wholly dedicated to the pursuit of railway history and the railway experience. This remarkable photograph shows a group of the country's foremost railway photographers in action at Camden, north London, probably in the 1950s. Many of the photographs that these men took are now in important railway collections, including that of the National Railway Museum in York. From left to right: CCB Herbert, CRL Coles, M Pinder, ED Bruton, W Bell, and MW Earley.

► While trainspotting was often a solitary activity, railway enthusiasm was widespread, resulting in the setting up of railway clubs all over Britain, with members of all ages. School railway clubs enabled many pupils to share their interests and to undertake activities that otherwise would have been inaccessible. This photograph, taken in the 1950s, shows a school group on a visit to a shed or depot, making the most of this 0-6-0 goods locomotive.

◄ As the rural railway, and the steam locomotive, came increasingly under threat, so railway clubs and similar organizations began to charter special rail tours dedicated to the exploration of threatened routes, preferably in historic vehicles. As a noted publisher of railway books, David & Charles arranged a number of such tours for their staff and other enthusiasts. This shows one such an outing, organized in May 1974 for the Booksellers Association (the bespectacled gentleman on the right is the co-founder and former owner of David & Charles, David St John Thomas).

TUNNELS

Tunnels are one of the most remarkable features of the railway age, representing as they do great engineering and astonishing feats of construction. Until the 1860s, railway engineers used the tunnelling technology of the 18th-century canal age, and every one was built by hand. The earliest railways, the Canterbury & Whitstable, the Liverpool & Manchester and the Leicester & Swannington, had tunnels on their routes, and the rapid expansion of the network brought hundreds more into being. In the end, there were about 1,060 tunnels in Britain, the longest of which is the one under the Severn, whose bore, four miles 628yd long, took 14 years to build. Another eight are over two miles long. Fifty are over a mile long. The deepest is Cowburn in Derbyshire, 875ft below the surface. The closing of lines inevitably resulted in many tunnels going out of use, but the durability of their structure meant that most survived. A few have been given new lives, as shooting ranges, for storage, and for the cultivation of mushrooms. Some have been taken over by bats and are, as a result,

▲ In 1956 a local stopping train makes its way through Miller's Dale, following the old Midland Railway's line through the Derbyshire hills, a route notable for viaducts and tunnels. The line closed in 1968.

In an image that captures totally the lure of the abandoned tunnel, three children pose below the ancient stone portal of Haie Hill tunnel, in the Forest of Dean, in August 1967, just a couple of weeks after the line's closure.

◀ Catesby tunnel was completed in 1897, on the Great Central's route through Northamptonshire. Over a mile long, the tunnel was closed with much of the former GCR route in 1966. The elegant engineering-brick portals have since been sealed up.

protected. Many have been sealed up and are inaccessible, but plenty remain open and can be explored by walkers and railway enthusiasts. Some are even on official footpaths and cycle routes. There is something particularly appealing about exploring a disused railway tunnel – a sense of history, an appreciation of the efforts of the men who built it, and the sheer excitement of the voyage through the dark.

▶ In tunnel terms, few names are more famous than Woodhead. Carved through the Pennines on the line between Sheffield and Manchester, the first tunnel, more than 3 miles long, was one of the great epics of early railway history. Completed in 1845, it was followed by a second, parallel tunnel in 1852. Just over a century later, both these single-track tunnels were replaced by a massive new bore, 27ft wide and 20ft high. Here, a freight train enters one of the castellated portals of the old tunnels. The whole route was closed in 1981, but reopening remains a possibility.

◀ A group of serious-looking and surprisingly well-dressed enthusiasts emerge from the mouth of Glenfield tunnel, on the Leicester and Swannington Railway, operated in 1832. Nearly everyone has a tie and a smart haircut. The only woman present is well to the rear.

◀ A long-abandoned tunnel and its approach cutting, overgrown and hidden in woods, is often an evocative sight, hinting at closure centuries rather than decades ago. This one is near the site of Lydbrook Junction, in the Forest of Dean.

▼ Ventnor, at the end of the line from Ryde, was an unusual station on the southern shore of the Isle of Wight. It was set into a vast excavated area that looked like a quarry, and the approach was through a long tunnel under St Boniface Down. Emerging trains came straight to the platforms, surrounded by smoke and steam, as can be seen here. The station site and the tunnel, now bricked up, survive.

TURNTABLES

Locomotives, as well as some other vehicles, have, by their nature, always had to be turned, so turntables of one kind or another have been associated with stations, engine sheds and goods yards since the 1830s. Initially quite primitive, these became more sophisticated as locomotives increased in size and weight and, from the 1870s, the standard turntable was set in a pit and balanced on a central pivot, with outer guiding wheels. Initially locomotives

▲ In the summer of 1953 a Southern Region Merchant Navy class locomotive no. 35026, 'Lamport & Holt Line', is slowly driven from the remarkably overgrown siding on to the turntable at Folkestone. Meanwhile, crew and some shed staff take a breather.

▼ By 1936, when this photograph was taken, turntables were often mechanically operated. However, at many places the application of manpower was still the only way to turn a locomotive. Here, at York, the crew struggle to turn no. 5093, a new-looking Stanier Black

were pushed round by their crews, but larger turntables demanded mechanical operation by electricity or via the locomotive's own vacuum braking system. Another turning system used a dedicated triangle of track.

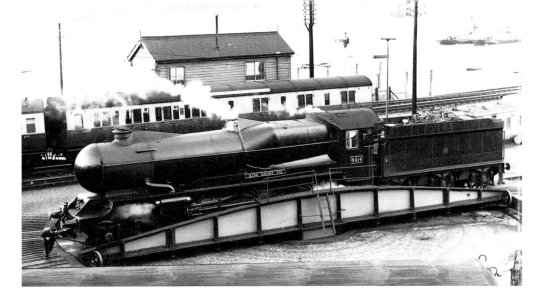

► Every terminus station of significance had to have turntable. This is Kingswear, Devon, in November 935, as GWR King class no. 6014 'King Henry VII' is owly turned by hand. The locomotive is carrying its hort-lived and rather ungainly streamlining.

◄ In May 1966 the steam age is nearing its end and turntable use is becoming a bit of a novelty. Spectators have gathered at Salisbury to watch Southern U class no. 31639 being turned after working an enthusiasts' special.

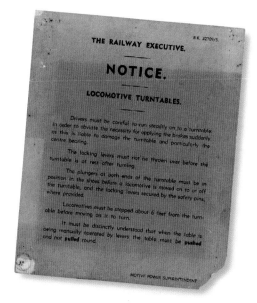

B.R. 32709/5

THE RAILWAY EXECUTIVE.

NOTICE.

LOCOMOTIVE TURNTABLES.

Drivers must be careful to run steadily on to a turntable in order to obviate the necessity for applying the brakes suddenly as this is liable to damage the turntable and particularly the centre bearing.

The locking levers must not be thrown over before the turntable is at rest after turning.

The plungers at both ends of the turntable must be in position in the shoes before a locomotive is moved on to or off the turntable, and the locking levers secured by the safety pins, where provided.

Locomotives must be stopped about 6 feet from the turntable before moving on to it to turn.

It must be distinctly understood that when the table is being manually operated by levers the table must be **pushed** and not **pulled** round.

MOTIVE POWER SUPERINTENDENT

◄ The alternative to a turntable was a dedicated triangle of track. This one is at Woodford Halse, on the Great Central line, in 1963, with a good crop of dandelions in flower. Today, few turntables survive in use, so preserved locomotives on mainline specials use triangles or run tender-first.

UNDERGROUND AND OVERGROUND

A feature of the late Victorian period was the rapid expansion of public transport in towns and cities. From the 1890s electric tramways were being built all over Britain. In London and Glasgow electric underground railways were running in deep-bored tunnels while Queen Victoria was still on the throne. The older cut-and-cover lines had been built from the 1860s, but deep tunnelling and electric power represented the new technology. The London underground was to be greatly expanded during the Edwardian period, with much of the modern network in the centre of London in place before World War I. In the United States and France there was a preference for elevated urban railways, but in Britain only Liverpool took this route in any significant way with the building from 1893 of the first six miles of the Liverpool Overhead Railway.

▶ The Liverpool Overhead Railway was the first electric urban system in the world and the first with automated signalling. These two photographs, taken in 1910, show the relationship between the railway and Liverpool's extensive docks. It was built 16ft above street level to facilitate access to the docks and to transport the thousands who worked there. The original line, from Dingle to Seaforth, had been extended by then to meet the Lancashire & Yorkshire lines to Southport and Ormskirk. Electric power was used to reduce the risk of fire in the warehouses.

Overhead Railway
Liverpool.

◀ This card, postmarked 1910, shows the popularity of the Overhead Railway, and the efficient service it offered. Never part of the nationalized network, it remained in use until 1956.

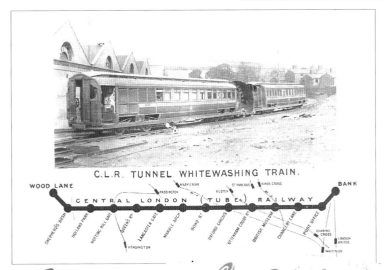

▲ Many London underground stations have changed their names. This is an Edwardian view of the entrance to Post Office station, on the Central London Railway, now St Paul's station, on the Central Line.

► Underground railway companies had many specialized vehicles to carry out maintenance at night or when the system was closed to the public. This Edwardian Central London promotional card shows a tunnel-whitewashing train, something unimaginable on today's London underground network.

► Nowadays dogs travel free on the London underground.

The Metropolitan was an independent railway with a large suburban network. It had freight and parcels facilities and even, on some services, Pullman cars. Electrified from 1905, it had distinctive locomotives and carriages, yet became a part of the London Transport underground network from 1933, while retaining its look and identity. Today it is just the Metropolitan line.

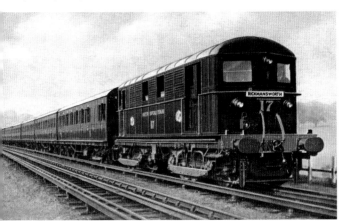

► This 1908 map, geographical rather than diagrammatic, shows much of the central London underground network in place and is therefore recognizable today. However, there have been changes. At least four stations on the map, Brompton Road, Down Street, York Road and Castle Road, no longer exist. Others have been renamed: Dover Street is now called Green Park, Great Central is Marylebone, Gillespie Road is Arsenal, Euston Road is Warren Street, British Museum is Holborn.

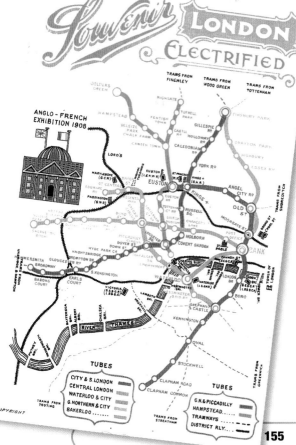

UNDERTAKERS

The funeral train, marking the final journey of notable figures, and in particular members of the royal family, is one of many special services developed during the 19th century. After Queen Victoria's death at Osborne House, on the Isle of Wight, in January 1901, her body was transported to the mainland on the royal yacht. From the private station at Gosport, she then travelled to London for the lying-in-state and funeral. Another rail journey followed for the burial at Windsor.

In less exalted circumstances, coffins were frequently transported by train on regular services, usually in the guard's van. In 1854 a large cemetery was set up at Brookwood, near Woking, in Surrey, by the London Necropolis Company. A funeral train ran there daily from the grand Waterloo Necropolis station, where mourners could gather before boarding the train. This soon proved popular, and services were maintained until World War II.

S 2409

THE STATION. BROOKWOOD CEMETERY.

▲ In the early 1920s a funeral train from Waterloo steams slowly into one of the two special stations at Brookwood – an unexpected scene to find on a postcard. The Necropolis Company supplied the hearse vans but services were operated initially by the LSWR and later by the Southern Railway.

▼ The railway funeral is staging a comeback, with a few preserved lines now offering special trains and services. The Midland Railway Centre in Debyshire, in conjunction with Peace Burials of Ormskirk, offers a package that includes a wicker coffin, a steam-hauled final journey and a burial spot within sight of the railway. Many enthusiasts have their ashes scattered by the line or put into the engine's firebox.

◄ ▼▼ Sir Winston Churchill, who died in January 1965, was probably the last Briton to have a great railway funeral. After its journey up the Thames, his coffin was loaded on to the train at Waterloo station, watched by members of his family. The Pullman train, headed by the Battle of Britain class locomotive that carried his name, then headed westwards, through the rain, towards Oxfordshire. No. 34051 'Winston Churchill' was subsequently preserved and now forms part of the National Railway Museum collection at York.

'Battle of Britain' Class Locomotive, "Winston Churchill" BY PERMISSION OF BRITISH RAILWAYS
3365

► Other monarchs followed the precedent set by Queen Victoria and were carried to their burial places in royal funeral trains, though generally with less complex journeys than hers. King Edward VII, Queen Victoria's son, died only nine years after her, in 1910. Here, on 20 May, crowds line the track as his royal funeral train passes through Ealing, in west London, on its journey to Windsor.

VIADUCTS

The viaduct is the most dramatic of all railway structures, and the one that makes the most enduring impact on the landscape. All over Britain, long after the lines have been closed, many still stand. The engineering principles had been well understood for centuries, but nothing of any significant size was built in Britain until the railway age, when large viaducts, mostly of brick or stone, suddenly proliferated. Early examples include Stephenson's Sankey viaduct on the Liverpool & Manchester Railway, whose eight arches were completed in 1830, and Buck's 27-arched Stockport viaduct of 1842.

In many cases viaducts were chosen in preference to embankments on grounds of cost and stability. In theory the number of arches could be unlimited. Britain's longest, at 1,275 yards, is the Welland in Rutland, completed in 1879. The best viaducts are defined by the height and curve of the arch and the thinness of the piers, and in many cases they achieve an elegance unusual in an engineering structure of such a scale. Brick and stone were the favoured materials, often used in conjunction with iron trusses. At first cast iron was employed but fears about stability inspired a switch to wrought

▲ The Pennine landscape of Yorkshire made many demands upon the railway builders, and tunnels and viaducts abound. The best viaduct is probably Sir John Hawkshaw's Lockwood viaduct near Huddersfield, whose 32 arches were completed in 1850. This old postcard view shows how the narrowness of the arches seems to increase the sense of height (actually 122 ft at the highest point).

◄ One of Britain's best-known viaducts is Ribblehead on the Settle & Carlisle line, which opened in 1876. Its superb setting is apparent here, as the 24 arches carry the streamlined A4 'Sir Nigel Gresley' more than 100 ft above the river valley.

► Knaresborough, in Yorkshire, is famous for its castle, high above the river Nidd, but the most frequently seen view of the town and river is this one, showing the viaduct. Completed in 1851, its four tall arches in decorative stone dominate both the town and the riverside. The architect, Thomas Grainger, took pains to make it blend with its surroundings. During its construction the viaduct collapsed and had to be rebuilt, delaying the opening of the line for three years. Such events, usually caused by poor workmanship, were not uncommon.

iron from the late 1840s. Brunel's use of timber for many viaducts in Devon and Cornwall was unusual, the last of which remained in service until 1934. Concrete, as blockwork or cast in situ, was used from the 1890s, with the 21 arches of Scotland's Glenfinnan being a particularly impressive example.

◄ Viaducts are a major feature of the line westwards from Plymouth to Penzance. Many were originally built from timber, to Brunel's designs, and from the late Victorian period onwards were gradually replaced. Today, their diversity, in terms of structure as well as landscape setting, adds greatly to the pleasures of the journey. Here, a modern Virgin train crosses the Largin viaduct.

WAITING ROOMS

WAITING · AND
LADIES ROOMS

Early railway companies often treated their passengers without much care or attention, and few stations offered any degree of comfort. If waiting rooms were provided they were generally gloomy and ill-equipped places. Indeed, the novelist Anthony Trollope described the facilities at Taunton as 'hideous, dirty and disagreeable'.

By the middle of the 19th century improvements had been made, and large stations often had a sequence of waiting rooms, catering for first, second and third class passengers, and separate areas for women. Smaller stations offered three rooms, first class, ladies, and general, and even on the smallest stations there was usually a separate room for ladies, something that has survived in a few places to the present day. There were also lavatories for ladies and gentlemen from an early date, sometimes combined with waiting rooms, and these were among the first public lavatories in Britain.

Standards varied considerably. At the worst, the waiting room was an open-fronted wooden shed with a hard bench, at the best there were upholstered seats, pictures and posters on the walls and, in winter, a roaring fire, features that made waiting for a train a relaxed and pleasant experience. Some stations had private waiting rooms, notably those used by the royal family and certain members of the aristocracy and their visitors. At Wolferton, the station for Sandringham, there were three royal waiting rooms. In recent years the waiting room has started to disappear, particularly at major stations, where it has been replaced by open seating on the concourse. By the same token, it was British Rail that started the logical process of merging the waiting room and the buffet.

▼ Farrington Gurney was a halt on the GWR line from Radstock to Bristol via Pensford. It had one platform and the most basic of waiting rooms. There was a separate ticket office, in a little room behind the Miner's Arms public house. On this grey day in the 1930s a single, smartly dressed passenger waits, preferring the platform to the wooden shelter

▲ Shepton Mallet Charlton Road station was on the Somerset & Dorset line. The gentlemen's lavatory looks pretty basic and seems to have faced out on to the platform. However, when travellers depended on station lavatories this was better than nothing.

In about 1910 an amateur photographer took this ocative view of passengers waiting at London's Holborn aduct station. A sailor sleeps on his kitbag and two en are in desultory conversation on benches that are rprisingly near to the platform edge. Even the South stern & Chatham locomotives seem to be waiting for mething to happen.

▼ Maidenhead acquired a new waiting room in 1943, a fully-glazed structure in the centre of the platform. The clearly visible interior made it safe for women, who on this station had to share the room with male travellers. At that time this was an unusual situation in larger stations.

▲ Waiting rooms today are relative rarities so passengers tend to wait on the platforms, taking advantage of the new generation of steel station benches. This is Malton in 2005, where most of the buildings are closed or given over to other purposes. Quite a crowd is waiting for the train to York.

WEATHER

ailways have always have been blighted by snow. Drifts block lines and derail trains, and even a minor fall can cause problems with signals and points and hinder staff movements, creating delays and cancellations. A number of serious accidents have been caused directly by snow, for example the collision at Abbots Ripton, near Huntingdon, in 1876. In severe winters, lines crossing rugged terrain have often been closed for days, while the notably bad winters of 1947 and 1963 resulted in weeks of disruption. More recently, in 1991, the railways became a national laughing stock when managers blamed delays on 'the wrong kind of snow'. Many lines, stations and other structures have also been damaged or destroyed by flooding. Swollen rivers frequently cause widespread inundations, while torrential rain and flash floods can cause landslides and destroy bridges, for example the Ness crossing, north of Inverness, swept away in 1989.

▼ It is the winter of 1947 and train services all over Britain face weeks of disruption. Drifting snow has brought traffic to a complete halt at Beaufort, a station in the Welsh Marches serving a mining community.

Some areas are prone to regular flooding, for example parts of Somerset. Here, in about 1910 Langport West on the Great Western line from Yeovil to Taunton, the track has become a river but, remarkably, the services are still operating and the crowds watch with interest the approaching train's bow wave.

In February 1971 the Cornish Riviera Express, under the control of a class 47 diesel locomotive, passes through Midgham station, near Newbury, fighting its way towards Paddington a violent snowstorm.

▶ Staff at St Bees on the Cumbrian Coast line near Whitehaven take a break from platform-clearing duties after a big snowfall in the 1890s. However, the drifts between the platforms will stop the trains running.

WORKS

The first factory set up to manufacture railway locomotives was opened by Robert Stephenson in 1823. Many others quickly followed. Famous names among the independent operators soon in the business included Vulcan Foundry, Sharp Stewart, Avonside, Hunslet, Beyer Peacock, and Andrew Barclay. The railway companies, too, built factories at their construction and maintenance works: during the Victorian period locomotives were being made in at least 25 works, the best known being Darlington, Doncaster, Derby, Crewe, Swindon and Ashford.

In 1900 British manufacturers were producing some 2,000 locomotives a year, selling them all over the world. Other companies specialized in rolling stock. Following the 1923 Grouping, some rationalization took place, a pattern followed after the setting up of British Railways. By now the emphasis was on diesel and electric traction, and the last mainline steam locomotive, 'Evening Star', left the Swindon works in 1960. Today few railway vehicles are built in Britain, but the independent operators have opened new maintenance facilities.

▶ During World War II many women replaced men in the workshops: in 1942 this machinist was photographed working for the Southern Railway.

◄ Many railway works focused on maintenance rather than building new vehicles. During a lifetime, apart from regular maintenance, a locomotive may have several refurbishments. This photograph shows class 31 and class 50 diesel locomotives, some dating to the 1960s, being totally rebuilt at the Doncaster works in 1984.

◄ In 1937, 100 new steam locomotives were built at the Darlington works for the LNER, part of a major modernization programme. Here, some of the wheel-sets for these locomotives are assembled and inspected.

▼ The Midland Railway's works at Derby, established from 1873, is one of the best-known in Britain, and one of the few still in operation. This view shows the erecting shop in LMS days.

CMX/595 (HD)

CONDUCTED TOUR
OF
DERBY LOCOMOTIVE WORKS

TUESDAY 25th AUGUST 1964

For Historical Notes on the journey from ST. PANCRAS see overleaf.

INCLUSIVE FARES
RAIL FARE AND TOUR OF LOCOMOTIVE WORKS

ADULTS		From	CHILDREN 12–14 years
s. d.			s. d.
26/-		ST. PANCRAS	13/-
24/-		ST. ALBANS City	12/-
22/-		LUTON Midland Road	11/-
17/9		BEDFORD Midland Road	9/-

CHILDREN UNDER 12 YEARS OF AGE NOT PERMITTED
CHILDREN 12—14 YEARS OF AGE MUST BE ACCOMPANIED BY AN ADULT.

OUTWARD							RETURN SAME DAY	
a.m.								
10 40	Depart	ST. PANCRAS				Arrive		
11 14	"	ST. ALBANS City					9 35	
11 30	"	LUTON Midland Road					8 52	
11 57	"	BEDFORD Midland Road					8 36	
p.m.								8 04	
1 52	Arrive	DERBY Midland				Depart	6 15	

REFRESHMENTS AVAILABLE ON THE TRAIN

BOOK EARLY TO AVOID DISAPPOINTMENT!

ACCOMMODATION ON THIS TRAIN IS LIMITED AND TICKETS CAN ONLY BE OBTAINED FROM THE BOOKING OFFICES AT THE ABOVE STATIONS OR BY PRIOR APPLICATION AT STATIONS, TOWN OFFICES OR OFFICIAL RAILWAY AGENTS.

Further information will be supplied on application to Stations, Official Railway Manager, St. Pancras Chambers, London, N.W.1 (Telephone: Euston 7070).

British Railways will be pleased to arrange for a representative to call upon secretaries or organisers respecting this excursion or any other outing.

British Railways
LONDON MIDLAND REGION

PLEASE RETAIN THIS BILL FOR REFERENCE   25 JUL 1964

eXCURSIONS

From the 1840s until the last years of British Rail, excursions formed a significant part of regular railway business. Over many decades individual companies, and then the various regions of the nationalized network, competed fiercely in the pursuit of custom. Most excursions were simply to resorts or places of interest, but many were more adventurous, combining train travel with coach tours or river and sea trips. Those with special interests, such as walkers, sports enthusiasts, nature lovers, photographers or shoppers, were also catered for. Some excursions were timed to coincide with regular holiday periods, such as Wakes Weeks, while others tried to make the most of

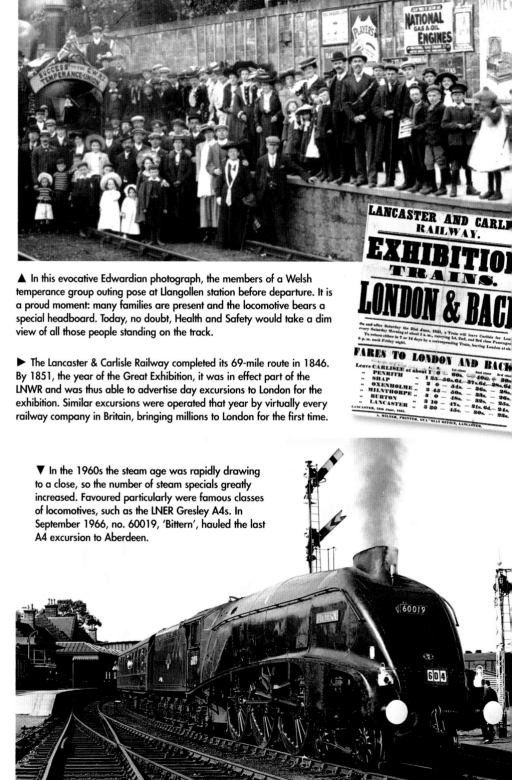

▲ In this evocative Edwardian photograph, the members of a Welsh temperance group outing pose at Llangollen station before departure. It is a proud moment: many families are present and the locomotive bears a special headboard. Today, no doubt, Health and Safety would take a dim view of all those people standing on the track.

▶ The Lancaster & Carlisle Railway completed its 69-mile route in 1846. By 1851, the year of the Great Exhibition, it was in effect part of the LNWR and was thus able to advertise day excursions to London for the exhibition. Similar excursions were operated that year by virtually every railway company in Britain, bringing millions to London for the first time.

▼ In the 1960s the steam age was rapidly drawing to a close, so the number of steam specials greatly increased. Favoured particularly were famous classes of locomotives, such as the LNER Gresley A4s. In September 1966, no. 60019, 'Bittern', hauled the last A4 excursion to Aberdeen.

◀ This Southern Railway booklet of 1928 shows that excursions to the coast were so regular they were almost in the timetable.

◄ Excursions taking railway enthusiasts on unusual journeys to remote parts of the network and little-used stations have always been popular. This predominantly male activity has occasionally involved families, as this 1950s photograph of a tour on the old Stafford to Uttoxeter line shows. The station is Chartley & Stowe, and everyone is probably watching the locomotive running round its train.

► Excursion marketing was often adventurous. This 1958 example offers 'a fascinating combination of events': an outing to Pitlochry to see the play *The Ghost Train*, hauled by a famous preserved steam locomotive.

▼ In 1961 an exceptionally long diesel multiple unit pauses at Woodburn en route from Blyth to Billingham, near Middlesbrough, for an agricultural show – a typical excursion special.

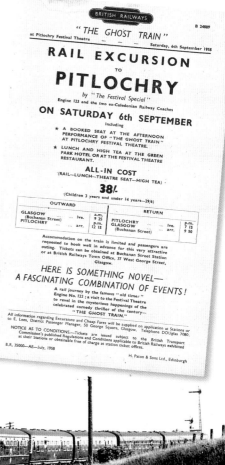

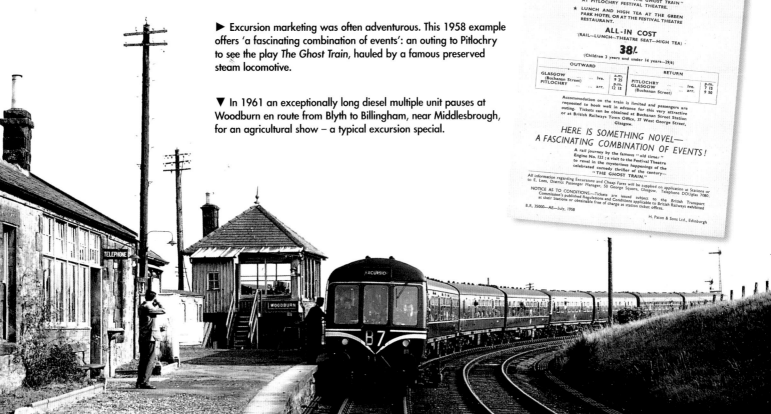

off-peak travel. There were also private excursions, run specially for groups or by companies for their employees. Also important throughout much of the 20th century were excursions run by or for rail enthusiasts, often featuring rare or unusual locomotives and vehicles or visiting remote parts of the network and lines threatened with closure.

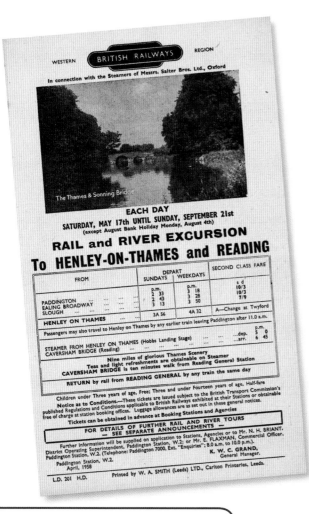

▲ The Cromford & High Peak Railway in Derbyshire, which closed in the 1960s, was primarily a freight line whose route featured fearsome inclines. Shortly before closure, these attracted many enthusiasts' specials.

◄ The combined rail and river trip was perennially popular, as underlined by this 1958 handbill. In this case, daily summer services were offered from London to Reading or Henley, with 'nine miles of glorious Thames Scenery'.

▶ This 1960 handbill was designed to attract the 'Stay-at-Home Holidaymakers', those who wanted to do their own thing during the official Edinburgh and Glasgow Trades Holiday period, from July to early September.

▶▶ In 1963 BR's Midland Region was organizing a series of conducted rambles in Derbyshire, Yorkshire and the Lakes. This handbill advertised rambles from soon-to-be-closed Tissington, along what is now famous as the Tissington Trail.

▼ Special interest groups were well catered for. Here, in 1958, an amateur photographers' special, organized in conjunction with the GWR, passes Pebworth Halt, probably on its way to or from Stratford-on-Avon.

For Stay-at-Home Holidaymakers

DURING THE WEEKS COMMENCING
4th, 11th, 18th and 25th JULY, 22nd and 29th AUGUST and 5th SEPTEMBER, 1960

SPECIAL
HOLIDAY RUNABOUT
RAIL TICKET
FOR
COAST and COUNTRY

BRITISH RAILWAYS

ORGANISED RAMBLES
FROM
TISSINGTON

(FOR ROUTES SEE OVER)
RAMBLES AVAILABLE FOR INDIVIDUALS AS WELL AS ORGANISED PARTIES.
LEADERS PROVIDED

Special Excursion
HARTINGTON   TISSINGTON   ASHBOURNE
SUNDAY 26th MAY 1963

FROM	Depart	SECOND CLASS RETURN FARES			Arrive Back
		Hartington	Tissington	Ashbourne	
	am	s d	s d	s d	pm
COLNE	8 30	12/9	14/-	14/9	11 27
NELSON	8 34	12/9	13/6	14/9	11 23
BRIERFIELD	8 37	12/6	13/6	14/6	11 19
BURNLEY Central	8 42	13/9	13/3	13/9	11 14
BURNLEY Barracks	8 45	11/9	13/3	13/9	11 11
ROSE GROVE	8 48	11/9	12/-	13/6	11 8
ACCRINGTON	8 56	10/6	12/-	12/9	11 0
CHURCH	8 59				
OSWALDTWISTLE	9 3	10/9	12/3	12/9	10 57
BLACKBURN	9 12	10/6	12/3	12/9	10 54
DARWEN	9 22	10/-	11/9	12/3	10 48
BOLTON	9 43	8/9	11/-	10/9	10 36
MANCHESTER Victoria	10 4	6/6	7/9	8/3	9 54
ARRIVAL TIMES		pm	pm	pm	
		12 0	12 32	12 48	
RETURN TIMES		pm	pm	pm	
		7 46	7 12	6 52	

Children under three years of age, free; three and under fourteen years of age, half-fare.

TICKETS CAN BE OBTAINED IN ADVANCE AT THE STATIONS AND OFFICIAL RAILWAY AGENTS

Further information will be supplied on application to the Stations, Official Railway Agents or to Mr. G. W. BRIMYARD, District Passenger Manager, L.M.R., Hunts Bank, Manchester 3, Tel. BLAckfriars 9456, Ext. 566.

LONDON MIDLAND   PLEASE SEE OVER

E292/HD

AMATEUR
PHOTOGRAPHERS
SPECIAL

YOUNG RAILWAYMEN

Detailed engineering models of trains exist from the early days of railways but, strangely, simple toys did not appear until the mid-19th century. The earliest examples, made in Germany from printed tin, were crude and had little in common with real trains. Train sets powered by clockwork, designed to run on rails rather than carpets, and accurately modelled, appeared at the end of the century, again mostly made in Germany. British-made sets were pioneered by Bassett-Lowke, but the real breakthrough came in the early 1920s when Frank Hornby launched his first 0-gauge trains, the start of an ever-expanding clockwork and electric range that brought railways into homes throughout the land. The smaller 00 gauge followed in the late 1930s, again inspired by Continental models. Since then the toy train has been an essential part of childhood. For many, the basic train set inspired a long-lasting passion for model railways, and a lifelong enthusiasm for the real thing.

▲ Model railways, and toy trains, come in all sizes and a varie of scales, the detail and finish determined by price. For most peopl the train set is laid out, played with and put away again, but othe build permanent layouts, often in a shed or the attic. Many als aspire to a garden railway. This 0-gauge Southern Railway exampl photographed in 1949, was clearly the owner's pride and jo

▶ From the 1920s to the 1960s Hornby offered a wonderful range of 0-gauge toy railways and accessories that made the most of the printed tin technology for which their Liverpool factory was so famous. This display suggests a terminus station at the end of a GWR branch line in Wales or the West Country, in the 1940s or 1950s.

◄ Model villages, popular tourist attractions since at least the 1920s, very often included model railways. This 1950s postcard shows a train crossing a fine bridge at Bekonscot Model Village in Beaconsfield, Buckinghamshire.

ALEXANDRA BRIDGE BEKONSCOT

▲ This charming Edwardian photograph shows a small boy with a magnificent toy train, including a goods wagon advertising the Eccles Co-Operative Society, a surprising touch in what is obviously a studio setting. It is likely the train was a photographer's prop, but the child seems more interested in the camera.

► Bassett-Lowke was one of the great names for toy trains and model engineering. Their extensive catalogues had much to offer the armchair enthusiast.

BASSETT-LOWKE LTᴅ

An Attractive All-purpose Model
STANDARD 6-COUPLED TANK

► Railway images were very popular in the 1920s and 1930s in children's books and as subjects for children's illustrations. Typical is this early card showing Bo-Peep and her sheep being firmly turned away from a toy train.

HORNBY-DUBLO
STATION NAMES

To be affixed to station nameboards
with Seccotine or cellulose adhesive

MECCANO LTD · ENGLAND

LICHFIELD LICHFIELD
OVERTON OVERTON
WESTBURY WESTBURY
NEWARK NEWARK
CRAWFORD CRAWFORD

Zoo on rails

The first railway to carry livestock was the Liverpool & Manchester Railway, in 1831. The trade expanded rapidly, becoming by the 1860s one of the mainstays of the network. In 1914 the railways transported more than 19 million sheep, cattle and pigs, and nearly 2,500 stations had livestock-handling facilities. Traffic diminished through the 20th century and the carriage of livestock finally ended in 1973. Other animal cargoes included horses, and notably racehorses, the transport of which continued in special vans into the 1960s. Large numbers of horses were also employed by the railways for haulage, transport and shunting duties. When British Railways was formed in 1948 it inherited over 9,000 horses, some of which worked until the 1960s. Smaller livestock included chickens and racing pigeons, the latter carried in huge quantities, at least until the 1970s, in special wagons for release by station staff at distant places. Dogs were frequent travellers, for decades needing their own tickets while cats and other small pets went free. And then there were the station pets, so many dogs, cats and tame birds kept by staff.

▲ Huge numbers of horses were employed by the railways for shunting duties, usually in country goods yards and small dock yards where locomotives were not always available. In these circumstances, the quickest and cheapest way to shunt single wagons was to use horsepower. This Edwardian view shows a more unusual sight, a horse being used to shunt a passenger coach in a large city station, in this case Lincoln.

▼ By 1965 livestock transport had greatly diminished, but animals were still carried in the guard's van from time to time. At Bailey Gate, on the Somerset & Dorset line, station staff struggle to force a reluctant stud ram on to the train.

It is a quiet day at Talybont-on-Usk in the summer of 1962 and the station is deserted except for a cow that has decided to take a walk along the platform after escaping, presumably, from the station's cattle pens.

Stations all over Britain had resident pets, usually cats or dogs. Here, staff at a small station pose for the camera: while the stationmaster hangs on to his cigar, one of his staff holds the pet mongrel.

▲ Station pets often enjoyed long lives, thanks to constant indulgence from staff and passengers. In death they were much lamented and well treated, as indicated by these pet graves at Talyllyn Junction.

INDEX

PICTURE CREDITS

Unless otherwise specified, all archive photographs and ephemera are from either the author's or the publisher's collections.

l = left; r = right; t = top; b = bottom;
m = middle
ABC Off By Train (published c.1946-47 by Raphael Tuck & Sons Ltd)
Ben Ashworth 2bl, 12/13b, 17bl, 27t, 38b, 59bl, 75tl, 75br, 82b, 94bl, 128l, 149r, 153bl, 173br
Associated Press 87ml
Paul Atterbury 12tr, 14bl, 14tr, 15tr, 16tl, 50b, 65r, 70b, 71bl, 76br, 78tl, 78tr, 78ml, 79br, 79mr, 99tl, 99b, 103ml, 104tr, 104b, 125bl, 160t
Hugh Ballantyne 11tl, 42tl, 86b, 98b, 98m, 125r, 145tl
A A F Bell 127tl
Tim Bleasdale 103bl
S V Blencowe Collection 147tl
Brighton Herald 2tr
A W Burges 9b
C L Caddy 45tr
D E Canning 129t, 162/163
I S Carr 99ml
H C Casserley 90tr, 167tl
Christie's Images 48b, 49tr, 60tr
C R L Coles 6/7, 13m, 54bl, 91b
Colour Rail 5tl, 19t, 39br, 42b, 57b, 58/59t, 60b, 69, 97tl, 123b, 127b, 135t, 138b, 157ml
C W Coslin 130tr
Derek Cross 53tl, 128tr
Kenneth Field 79tl, 85, 150tr
J A Fleming 87br
T G Flinders 78bl
P J Fowler 112b, 146bl
John Goss 52bl, 55tl, 82r, 84br, 110/111, 131r
Tony Harden 5tr, 25tr, 38tr, 100m, 100tr, 101br, 119tr, 121tl, 155tl, 155br, 155tr, 156tr, 165b
G T Heavyside 30tr, 45b
Julian Holland 6/7, 15m, 56B, 57tr, 95tr, 143tl, 151tl, 170b
Robert Humm 131bl
Derek Huntriss 158/159t, 159bl, 168t
Ivo Peters Collection 26br, 48tr, 129r, 137br, 137tr
Alan Jarvis 6/7, 40/41b, 56t, 70tr, 74b, 77ml, 78mr, 109r, 109tl, 151b, 172br, 173t
M A King 133b
Kevin Lane 136tr
Locomotive & General 113b, 141br
Mark Blencowe Collection 76bl
Colin Marsden 138tr
Michael Mensing 36/37b, 52tr, 74tr, 148b, 148/149t, 196b
Midland Railway Centre 156b
Gavin Morrison 4tr, 6/7, 14/15b, 61tr, 71tl, 71r, 94tr, 96bl, 109bl, 123t, 124t, 134b, 144br, 159tr, 164tr
Newcastle Chronicle & Journal 85tr, 86 (Insets)
Neville Stead Collection (BG Tweed) 92tr
Peter Oliver (David Spaven Collection) 41tr
Photomatic 26tr
C Plant 54tr
Post Office 83b
R C Riley 6/7, 11b, 69br, 129bl
Gerald T Robinson 77tl
E H Sawford 44b, 152tr
Science & Society Photo Library 20/21, 46bl, 47, 47mr, 143m, 160b, 161tl, 161bl
Sealink (BRB) 119br
W S Sellar 166br, 167b
Brian Sharpe 19b, 49bl, 126, 136bl
Frank Spaven (David Spaven Collection) 25t, 103t
A E Staples 144tr
Andrew Swift 10b, 20bl, 31t, 32br, 33t, 88b, 89b, 89ml, 92b, 93br, 95br, 101br, 102tr, 140bl, 142bl, 162tr, 162bl, 166tr, 172tr
Douglas Thompson 75tr
Mike Turner 42mr
R E Tustin 170tr

THE AUTHOR

Paul Atterbury is a lifelong railway enthusiast who has always appreciated the power of railway ephemera – such as postcards, timetables and ticke– to tell the story of Britain's railway past. Familiar to many as a long-standing member of the team of experts on BBC TV's *Antiques Roadshow*, Paul's previous railway books include *Discovering Britain's Lost Railways*, *Branch Line Britain*, *Along Country Lines*, *Tickets Please!* and *Along Lost Lines, All Change* and *Life Along the Line*.